# FORENSICS
## in CHEMISTRY

*The Case of Kirsten K.*

# FORENSICS in CHEMISTRY

## The Case of Kirsten K.

Sara McCubbins
and Angela Codron

NSTApress
National Science Teachers Association
Arlington, Virginia

National Science Teachers Association

Claire Reinburg, Director
Jennifer Horak, Managing Editor
Andrew Cooke, Senior Editor
Wendy Rubin, Associate Editor
Agnes Bannigan, Associate Editor
Amy America, Book Acquisitions Coordinator

ART AND DESIGN
Will Thomas Jr., Director
Lucio Bracamontes, Graphic Designer
Cover photography by Talaj for iStock

PRINTING AND PRODUCTION
Catherine Lorrain, Director
Jack Parker, Electronic Prepress Technician

NATIONAL SCIENCE TEACHERS ASSOCIATION
Francis Q. Eberle, PhD, Executive Director
David Beacom, Publisher

1840 Wilson Blvd., Arlington, VA 22201
*www.nsta.org/store*
For customer service inquiries, please call 800-277-5300.

NSTA is committed to publishing material that promotes the best in inquiry-based science education. However, conditions of actual use may vary, and the safety procedures and practices described in this book are intended to serve only as a guide. Additional precautionary measures may be required. NSTA and the authors do not warrant or represent that the procedures and practices in this book meet any safety code or standard of federal, state, or local regulations. NSTA and the authors disclaim any liability for personal injury or damage to property arising out of or relating to the use of this book, including any of the recommendations, instructions, or materials contained therein.

PERMISSIONS
Book purchasers may photocopy, print, or e-mail up to five copies of an NSTA book chapter for personal use only; this does not include display or promotional use. Elementary, middle, and high school teachers may reproduce forms, sample documents, and single NSTA book chapters needed for classroom or noncommercial, professional-development use only. E-book buyers may download files to multiple personal devices but are prohibited from posting the files to third-party servers or websites, or from passing files to non-buyers. For additional permission to photocopy or use material electronically from this NSTA Press book, please contact the Copyright Clearance Center (CCC) (*www.copyright.com*; 978-750-8400). Please access *www.nsta.org/ permissions* for further information about NSTA's rights and permissions policies.

LIBRARY OF CONGRESS CATALOGING-IN-PUBLICATION DATA
McCubbins, Sara.
  Forensics in chemistry: the case of Kirsten K. / by Sara McCubbins and Angela Codron.
      p. cm.
  Includes bibliographical references.
  ISBN 978-1-936137-36-7—ISBN 978-1-936959-83-9 (e-book) 1. Chemistry, Forensic—Study and teaching (Secondary) I. Codron, Angela. II. Title.
  HV8073.M3325 2012
  363.25071'2—dc23
                2011049549

# Contents

# CONTENTS

# ABOUT THE AUTHORS

**Sara A. McCubbins,** M.S., is a project and office manager for the Center for Mathematics, Science, and Technology (CeMaST) and an instructor and advisor in chemistry education at Illinois State University. Her interests include curriculum development, professional development for teachers, university and community outreach, analyzing the role informal science plays in scientific knowledge acquisition, and student attitudes toward science.

**Angela R. Codron** is currently a chemistry and biology teacher at Normal West High School in Normal, Illinois. Her educational experiences range from an undergraduate degree in chemistry eeducation to a Master's in athletic administration, both from Eastern Illinois University, and a Type 75 Educational Administration Certificate from Illinois State University. Her areas of interest in education include developing and incorporating performance-based assessments for use in the science classroom and aligning and assessing curriculum with specific learning targets.

# ACKNOWLEDGMENTS

As with any large-scale project, this work owes a great deal to many individuals and organizations. The authors would like to recognize the Center for Mathematics, Science, and Technology (CeMaST) at Illinois State University for its continued support of this project; Dr. William Hunter, director of CeMaST, for his guidance and support; Abby Newcomb and Mary McCubbins, for their help in testing some of the curriculum; Amanda Fain, for her editing; Dr. Darci Harland, for her guidance in the proposal process; and Mary McCubbins, for her uncanny ability to take what was written and create meaningful graphics.

We also wish to thank the science department and the administration at Normal Community West High School for their continued support of curriculum that revolves around performance-based assessments and for allowing its science classrooms to be a true laboratory for learning. A special thank you to the Chemistry II students who have readily participated in these assessments; without their feedback and patience these assessments would not be as successful as they are in the classroom.

This body of work was the result of the Partnerships for Research in Science and Mathematics education (PRISM) Project, a program that originated in 2001 and was supported by the National Science Foundation grant 0086354 from the Graduate Teaching Fellows in K–12 Education program.

Sara McCubbins would like to thank the following people: Mrs. Angie Lawrence, for first planting the seed and teaching me to truly love science; Ms. Lisa Thomas, who taught me to love both science *and* writing—after all, you were the first to call me *Sara, the Writer*; Dr. William Hunter, not only for cultivating that love of science and writing, but also for always daring me to dream bigger; Ms. Angie Codron, for showing me what true inquiry in the classroom looks like, and for always saying "yes" to any harebrained ideas we might dream up—you are a true friend, and the partnership we have developed over the years can only lead to great things; and to my family and friends, who continue to support me and encourage me always to pursue my passions.

Angela Codron would like to thank the following people: the science department at St. Charles North High School for helping engrain the value of performance based assessment in curriculum planning during her first year of teaching; Dr. William Hunter, for believing in the importance of science education and the use of unique instruction for

# ACKNOWLEDGMENTS

maximum student learning; Ms. Elisa Palmer and Ms. Darci Harland for the inspiration to use biology based forensics and transform it for my chemistry classroom; Ms. Sara McCubbins, for providing the spark for me to begin to share what I do in the classroom and helping me have the confidence to think others would really be interested in it; and my family for supporting the task of writing a book and allowing me to cross one more thing off my list of things to accomplish in my career.

## NSTA PRESS EXTRAS

On the NSTA Press Extras page for *Forensics in Chemistry* you will find downloadable PDFs for student assessment handouts, teacher guides, and grading rubrics for each lesson in the book. Please visit *www.nsta.org/publications/press/extras/kirstenk.aspx*.

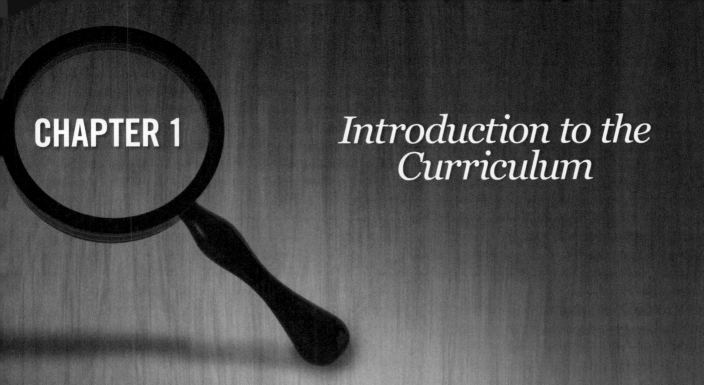

# CHAPTER 1

# Introduction to the Curriculum

The curriculum presented in this book was built on the foundation of performance-based assessments, which are used to measure content knowledge and skills in the chemistry classroom. As a teacher, I often struggled to make high-level chemistry topics—such as Advanced Stoichiometry, Beer's Law, Nuclear Chemistry, Electrochemistry, Equilibrium, Acids and Bases, and Organic Chemistry—relevant to students. Through the use of forensics in *The Case of Kirsten K.*, we found a way to present these high-level topics to students in a meaningful way. By having students solve one piece of the forensics case at a time so that they solve the entire case by the end of the year, not only are we able to maintain student interest, but we also have the opportunity to bring chemistry as a whole into focus for the students.

## DEVELOPMENT OF THE PROJECT

The idea for the development of this chemistry-based forensic assessment project first stemmed from working with the Partnership for Research in Science and Mathematics Education (PRISM) program at Illinois State University (ISU). This program was funded by the GK–12 Fellows Program

from the National Science Foundation (NSF) to allow graduate students at ISU the opportunity and funding to work with classroom teachers to develop curriculum, lessons, or projects that the teachers would otherwise not have the time or resources to develop. I had worked with PRISM for about four years before I started working with then–graduate student Sara McCubbins. I approached Sara with the idea of creating a yearlong performance-based assessment for my Chemistry II class that would reinforce the high-level chemistry topics required in the course and relate it to forensics—something that would guarantee the students' interest. By linking the assessments to forensics, we felt students would make more connections between chemistry concepts that they may not be able to make on their own. We have presented this forensics-based assessment curriculum at the Illinois Science Teachers Association (ISTA) and National Science Teachers Association (NSTA) conferences in 2009, and with this book, we hope to make it more practical for classroom teachers to implement this type of assessment into their own classrooms.

Forensics has the unique ability to maintain student interest and promote content learning. Students' interests are immediately peaked, and forensics gave us all a common ground to revisit at the end of each unit. When you expand their minds with the use of creative assessments, students remember those activities long after they leave the classroom. I still have students approach me from past years and ask about the forensics case and specific characters from the story.

One way to develop meaningful understanding and interest in Science, Technology, Engineering, and Mathematics (STEM) concepts is through the application of those concepts to relevant issues (NRC 1996). The popularity of television shows such as *Bones, CSI,* and *Cold Case* have led to a documented increase of student interest in science and forensics (Bergslien 2006; Colgan 2002; Kaplan 1993; Smallwood 2002). This increased interest provides educators the perfect opportunity to use forensics in their classroom. In fact, "the nature of forensic science makes it ideal for attacking the problems of teaching science because students can practice science as inquiry" (Funkhouser and Deslich 2000). Because this forensics-based curriculum spans the entire school year, the students are able to use the skills learned in the classroom and apply them to the forensics case they are solving in the lab.

In addition to providing chemistry-based lessons exploring the topic of forensics, *The Case of Kirsten K.* also provides educators with the opportunity to highlight the competitive nature of the forensics field and the career opportunities it presents. According to the U.S. Department of Labor, the number of forensic science technicians is expected to increase by 20% between 2008 and 2018 (Bureau of Labor Statistics 2009). A large portion of this growth will be driven by the increased application of forensic science techniques by state and local government to examine, solve, and prevent crime. Providing students the opportunity to merge their science and chemistry skills with this growing field of study allows them to see the numerous career paths in which chemistry is applicable.

Some critics suggest that the topic of forensics in schools is being overused. While this may be true according to the resources available for the elementary and middle school levels, as well as the biological sciences, it is certainly not true for chemistry classes. And while many forensics activities and assessments exist for the high school science classroom individually, they are seldom able to link together multiple concepts throughout the year. Such activities are often treated as a "drop-in" unit or done for one assessment and then quickly forgotten. Even when educators use multiple forensics activities, the assessments are often unrelated. Kaplan explains that "a series of seemingly unrelated experiments illustrating unrelated concepts is not effective in stimulating student interest, capturing their attention, and motivating them toward further study in the sciences" (1993). The curriculum in this book is significant and unique because it includes multiple forensics-based chemistry assessments that are all linked together throughout the year.

In September 2000, John Funkhouser and Barbara J. Deslich published an article in *The Science Teacher* on how to integrate forensic science into the chemistry curriculum. They explained that there were two primary obstacles that impeded the ability for such programs to take root in classrooms. One of these obstacles was teacher confidence. The other was that "no complete source of information exists that is aimed at a high school level, much less a hands-on, inquiry-based descriptive text or manual." This book removes the second of those obstacles by providing an entire year's worth of chemistry curriculum centered on forensics that uses performance-based assessment strategies.

The concept of having students solve one piece of the puzzle at a time, so that they solve the case by the end of the year, not only maintains student interest, but also allows the students to see how the chemistry topics they learn throughout the year are all related to each other. *The Case of Kirsten K.* **does**

**not** replace an entire year's worth of chemistry curriculum! Rather, it highlights the chemistry content connections, which students often fail to notice, by incorporating forensics-based evidence into a series of labs spread throughout the year. In total, students complete eight hands-on labs that are directly linked to the forensics case. While each performance assessment could be easily modified and used individually, the intention is to use all the assessments in a yearlong project that continually connects complex chemistry curriculum into something that is more relatable to students and brings chemistry as a whole into focus.

## THE IMPORTANCE OF PERFORMANCE-BASED ASSESSMENT

In addition to teaching chemistry through the unique and interesting lens of a forensics case, this curriculum also uses a variety of teaching strategies and pedagogical tools that are considered to be best practice, such as performance-based assessment. Performance-based Assessments, or PBAs, have been shown to enhance long-term memory and student comprehension (Krovetz et al. 1993; Newmann and Wehlage 1993; Rutherford 1990; Wygoda and Teague 1995). The curriculum presented in this book was built on the foundation of performance-based assessments, which are used to measure content knowledge and skills in the chemistry classroom.

In *The Case of Kirsten K.*, students complete five different performance-based assessments throughout the year that are tied to this forensics case. Each PBA focuses on content covered from the previous unit and centers on one piece of the forensics crime. These PBAs often involve multiple stations where students are analyzing evidence. A typical PBA for this curriculum will last anywhere from three to five days in the lab. Considering the breadth of chemistry that the PBA is assessing, the weeklong timeframe is appropriate. Additionally, because students

are trying to solve a case, they often forget that the work they are doing is actually a way of assessing their chemistry content knowledge and skills, which makes this authentic assessment somewhat unique. Research in authentic assessment has shown that students are so involved that they voluntarily discuss the project with others, explaining what they are doing and why (Krovetz et al. 1993; Newmann and Wehlage 1993; Wygoda and Teague 1995). Evidence of this for *The Case of Kirsten K.* can be seen from the popularity of the course and continued high enrollment.

## PREPARING YOUR STUDENTS FOR INQUIRY LABS

In Appendix E, you will find an example of an inquiry-based lab that I use to prepare my students for the types of labs they will conduct throughout this forensics case. It is important that students learn the skill of reverse inquiry, so that they can look at crime scene data and work backward to figure out what the evidence means within the big picture of the case. The first day of school, I have the lab set up as if Dr. BrINClHOF (an acronym for the diatomic elements) has been working on several labs in my classroom over the summer. I approach the students, who are locked out of my room and are standing in the hallway, to tell them there has been a murder in our lab and police think it is Dr. BrINClHOF who has been murdered. Students already know about Dr. BrINClHOF because we learned about him in their first year of chemistry class. I tell students that police need their help in learning about what Dr. BrINClHOF could have been studying in the lab because it will help them solve the murder. I relate all the labs to the topic of greenhouse gases, the gas laws, and atmospheric pressure to lead students to learn that he was working in the lab studying climate change. The global climate change debate lends itself well to a murder forensics case because of its controversial nature. After completing this lab, students are well prepared for the performance-based assessments that will take place throughout the year and are excited to receive the first piece of the case in *The Case of Kirsten K.*

## REFERENCES

Bergslien, E. 2006. Teaching to avoid the "CSI effect": Keeping the science in forensic science. *Journal of Chemical Education* 83 (5): 690–691.

Bureau of Labor Statistics. 2009. *Occupational outlook handbook, 2010–11 edition, science technicians.* Available online at *www.bls.gov/oco/ocos115.htm*

Colgan, C. 2002. Teaching forensics, then and now. *Education Digest* 68 (1): 59–61.

Funkhouser, J., and B. J. Deslich. 2000. Integrating forensic science. *The Science Teacher* 67 (6): 32–35.

Kaplan, L. F. 1993. Forensic science: Crime in the chemistry curriculum: Projects supported by the NSF division of undergraduate education. *Journal of Chemical Education* 70: 574–575.

Krovetz, M., D. Casterson, C. McKowen, and T. Willis. 1993. Beyond show and tell. *Educational Leadership* 50 (7): 73–76.

National Research Council (NRC). 1996. *National science education standards.* Washington, DC: National Academies Press.

Newmann, F. M., and G. Wehlage. 1993. Five standards of authentic instruction. *Educational Leadership* 50 (7): 8–12.

Rutherford, F. J. 1990. *Science for all Americans.* New York: Oxford University Press.

Smallwood, S. 2002. As seen on TV. *Chronicle of Higher Education* 48 (45): A8–A10.

Wygoda, L., and R. Teague. 1995. Performance-based chemistry: Developing assessment strategies in high school chemistry. *Journal of Chemistry Education* 72 (10): 909–911.

# CHAPTER 2

# *The Big Picture*

Before delving into each individual activity presented in this text, it is important to understand an overall picture of the forensics case itself and what is expected of the students. This section will also explain how information is organized within this book to provide the most user-friendly teacher resource possible.

## DETAILS ABOUT THE CASE

Each performance assessment focuses on a different set of chemistry topics and chronologically follows the typical second-year chemistry curriculum. What follows is a brief description of each of the performance assessments that make up the entire yearlong forensics case.

- *The Cooler and Delivery Truck Evidence.* Students must use their knowledge of density to design an experiment that will determine which lake/creek sample(s) the blue plastic cooler pieces are from, based on the ability of the cooler pieces to float. In addition, students will use gas laws to determine details surrounding air bag deployment from the victim's delivery truck.

- *The Chemical Evidence.* This calculation-based activity has students identify chemical evidence from the crime scene (identified in *The Cooler and Delivery Truck Evidence*) based on the percentage of four distinct residues found.

- *The Nuclear Radiation Evidence.* In this assessment, students analyze nitrate levels in soil samples, gather quantitative and qualitative data on shoe prints found at the crime site, use their knowledge of radioactive decay to date four different fragments of bone found at the crime scene, and use beta decay calculations to develop a time frame for the murder.

A Spec-20 is needed for this assessment or Lab Quest with Spectro-Vis probe, but a "conviction" can still be achieved at the end of the year without this particular piece of evidence.

- *The Weapon Analysis.* During the first two parts of this assessment, students use fingerprint analysis and the electric potential for each gun and bullet combination to determine which subject matches each gun and which bullet came from the guns. In the final two parts, students will determine which suspects are positive for gunshot residue using titration techniques and also which clothing stains for each suspect are positive for human blood using pH values and calculations.

- *The Drug Lab Evidence.* Students must first use knowledge of organic functional groups and IR spectrometry to identify three known substances from the discovered drug lab. Then thin layer chromatography is used to identify the unknown drugs suspected of being sold and also to identify the pen used for writing in the drug sale transaction notebook. A caffeine extraction lab will also be performed to determine if caffeine was in fact being extracted from the coffee grounds found in the drug lab.

## THE COMPLETE SCENARIO

In the following chapters, you will find detailed information about each performance assessment and the evidence collected within that unit. However, we have provided a brief overview here to give you a better understanding of the case as a whole, including links between the suspects and victim.

### Evidence Gathered From the Cooler and Delivery Truck

Students should conclude that the suspect was not able to sink the cooler in any of the surrounding lakes, even with a body in it, a chain wrapped around it, and water filling it. For this reason, the suspect(s) had to take the cooler to a recycling plant to dispose of the evidence. When students create a density gradient, they should find that the blue cooler pieces

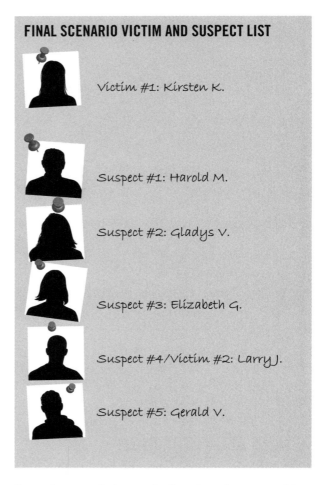

**FINAL SCENARIO VICTIM AND SUSPECT LIST**

Victim #1: Kirsten K.

Suspect #1: Harold M.

Suspect #2: Gladys V.

Suspect #3: Elizabeth G.

Suspect #4/Victim #2: Larry J.

Suspect #5: Gerald V.

from the recycled sample float in salt water with a density of 1.05g/ml and sink in vinegar with a density of 1.01 g/ml. The students should choose Clinton Lake as the lake where police should start looking because it has a slightly higher density than the other lakes (1.05g/ml), and this would have kept the blue cooler from sinking in that particular lake. Students should also conclude that the airbag volume of the sunken delivery truck will not exceed 65 L so it will not burst as the truck is removed from the lake and police will be able to collect further data on the airbag and within the truck.

The most probable suspects at this point, based on Suspect File A, would be Harold M. because he lives in Clinton and may know the area. The other suspect would be Gladys V. because she owns a house on the lake and would have direct access to Clinton Lake. Elizabeth G. may also be questioned in this case because she owns the wedding cake delivery truck that was found at the bottom of Clinton Lake. Police may want to look into records of regular maintenance done on the truck to see if it had any effect on the accident.

### Evidence Gathered From the Chemical Evidence

Students should find that while the body has not been discovered yet, plenty of evidence can be collected at the crime scene around the Clinton Lake area. The victim and suspects each had articles of clothing that the police collected to test for any chemical samples that matched those samples found at the crime scene. The victim's clothing was found to have vanilla ($C_8H_8O_3$) on it, which also matches a chemical found in the delivery truck and at the crime scene around Clinton Lake. This makes sense because she was last seen delivering a wedding cake, and she also worked at Elizabeth G.'s wedding cake business. Suspect #1, Harold M., was found to have aspirin ($C_9H_8O_4$) on him. This chemical was also found at the crime scene, but this is an over-the-counter drug and very common, so it doesn't necessarily place Harold directly at the crime scene. Suspect #2, Gladys V., had cocaine ($C_{17}H_{21}NO_4$) on her. This is suspicious for two reasons: (1) because cocaine is an illegal substance and (2) because it was also found at the crime scene. Gladys V. should be watched closely in future investigations.

Elizabeth G., Suspect #3, had acetaminophen on her and also a second chemical (unknown #1), which students learn later in this assessment is glyoxylic acid ($C_2H_2O_3$), a chemical used in the cake business to make vanilla. Acetaminophen is also an over-the-counter drug and was not found at the crime scene, so Elizabeth G. would not be a suspect at this time. Larry J. was found to have two chemicals

on him, nitroglycerine ($C_3H_5N_3O_9$) and an unknown #2 ($C_4H_5N_2O$), later to be identified as the empirical formula of caffeine (during the fourth performance assessment). Larry J. should be questioned further at this point because the unknown chemical found on him was also found at the crime scene.

Harold M. recently had surgery, which would explain the fact that he had aspirin, but it is still suspicious that aspirin was found at the crime scene as well. He also has a connection to the victim because he recently had back surgery and Kirsten K. was his nurse. The victim and her husband were renting the lake house from Gladys V. the week that Kirsten went missing. This and her illegal drug activity makes Gladys V. a prime suspect at this time. Larry J. also needs to be questioned further because of his prior convictions of drug charges and a possible connection to the cocaine found at the crime scene and on Gladys.

### Evidence Gathered From Nuclear Radiation

Students find out that the case of Kirsten K. has gone from a missing-persons case to a murder investigation. Students should find that Larry J. and Elizabeth G.'s shoes had nitrates on them that matched the soil sample from the area where the body was found. Students also should match shoe prints of the suspects' shoes to the shoe prints the police lifted from the crime scene. Every suspect's shoe prints were found at the crime scene except Harold M.'s. It is important for students to take into account where each shoe was found when they collect information from the forensic tag on each shoe. For example, Larry J.'s shoe was actually found in the trunk of Elizabeth G.'s car, and they were both seen leaving a restaurant together recently. Students should also find that Bone fragment #3 was the only one that could have possibly belonged to the victim because it is the only one that has not decayed at all into the daughter isotope. Students cannot do further testing on the bone, but they can recommend to the police that further testing be done. In the last part of the assessment, students find out that the victim was given a medical tracer to kill her. She was given 34.8 g of the tracer and the lethal dose is 30 g. Students should put together all the evidence at this point and conclude that while Kirsten K. was missing for several months, she was not killed until recently (about 24 days ago) based on the decay of the medical tracer found in her body.

The top suspects at this point would be Larry J. and Elizabeth G. The soil match and their recent activity—meeting at restaurants while Larry's wife is missing—seem suspicious. Also, there may be some talk around town about Larry J. and Elizabeth G. because her client number has decreased for her wedding cake business. Gladys V. has a lake house on Clinton Lake and she enjoys taking walks around the lake, so it may explain why her shoe prints would be found there. Also, Harold M. was hired to do some plumbing work at the lake house recently, but this is not necessarily suspicious since he lives in Clinton and his shoe prints were not found around the crime scene.

## Evidence Gathered From Weapon Analysis

Students should find that two fingerprints are on each gun handle. On the aluminum foil handle, the fingerprints are Larry J.'s and also an Unknown fingerprint that doesn't match any of the current suspects. On the copper foil handle, the fingerprints are Gladys V.'s and also the same Unknown fingerprint that matches the print on the aluminum foil handle. Students later find out that there is a new suspect, Gerald V., who is the son of Gladys V. Students also find that the aluminum foil gun fired the zinc bullet and the copper foil gun fired the silver bullets. The silver bullets were the ones found in Larry J.'s chest. Gladys V. tested negative for gunshot residue, so while Gladys V. may not have fired the gun, her prints are on it, probably trying to cover up the murder of Larry J. that her son committed by hiding the gun in the garbage can at the lake house. Larry J. and Gerald V. have both tested positive for gunshot

residue. Kirsten K., Larry J., Gladys V., and Gerald V. all tested positive for blood stains. Students should match up that Kirsten K. has her own blood on her; Larry J. had his own blood and also Gerald V.'s blood on him; and Gerald V. has his own blood, Larry J.'s blood, and Kirsten K.'s blood on him. This puts Gerald V. and Larry J. in a gun fight where Gerald V. murdered Larry J. and most likely is the one who kidnapped Kirsten K. and then killed her with his mother's help and her pharmacy connection to get the medical tracer. At this point the students don't really know why there was a gun fight and why Kirsten K. went missing and was then drugged to death. Students should be suspicious of what is going on in Gladys V.'s basement at the lake house since that is where Larry J. and Gerald V.'s gun fight took place. Harold M., Gladys V., and Gerald V. all are licensed gun owners and have deer permits, but this just may be a cover-up to protect what is really going on in the basement of the lake house. Harold M. and Elizabeth G. are no longer suspects in the murder. Larry J. may have been meeting with Elizabeth G. because she is a neighbor and a longtime friend and maybe he needed someone to talk with during the time when his wife was missing.

## Evidence Gathered From Drug Lab Evidence

Students learn that police have found some unknown, white, druglike substance in the basement of Gladys V.'s lake house. After further analysis of the basement, the students find that Gerald V. and his mother were trying to extract caffeine from coffee grounds to use in this drug being made in the basement. The drug is found to have both caffeine and aspirin in it, so it may be some type of ultra-powerful migraine medicine that they were selling without a prescription to make more money, since Gladys V. is recently retired from the pharmacy business. Also, Gladys V. had cocaine on her (identified in performance assessment #2), so they may have been making more than just this migraine medicine in the lake house basement. There was a drug log book that police were analyzing, and this book had Larry J.'s name in it several times. Since Larry was convicted of drug use previously, students should conclude that Larry J. may have owed Gerald V. money for past drug use, so Gerald V. kidnapped Kirsten K. to hold her for ransom to get the money he was owed. Gerald V. got impatient while waiting for his money so he killed Kirsten K. to show Larry J. how serious he was about getting his money. Larry J. may have been meeting with Elizabeth G. about getting a loan from the wedding cake business to pay off Gerald. After hearing that Kirsten K. had been murdered, Larry J. went over to Gerald V.'s to confront him and that is when the gun fight took place.

## CHAPTER ORGANIZATION

Each chapter will include case information specific to each performance assessment and will highlight the national standards and chemistry content addressed by each performance assessment. In addition, the remainder of each chapter will be organized in the following order:

1. *Teacher Guide:* A list of helpful teacher set-up tips, answers to questions, details about equipment set-ups, and what the students should expect as they investigate the evidence for each assessment.
2. *The Case of Kirsten K.:* The actual performance assessment that is handed to students at the end of the unit.
3. *Suspect File:* The introduction of the characters and new information about them and their relationship to the case being investigated.
4. *Student Lab Report Example:* A sample of student work that has been previously submitted and assessed. This will also serve as an answer key for teachers.

5. *Grading Rubric:* The actual grading rubric used for each assessment will be included and is created using the Applications of Learning Rubric in Appendix B.

## CHEMISTRY CONCEPTS CHART (APPENDIX A)

Each of the performance assessments listed in the chemistry concepts chart include the chemistry concepts covered, the questions raised with each piece of evidence presented, and the conclusions students should come to from the evidence collected.

## GRADING RUBRIC: NOTES TO THE TEACHER AND APPLICATIONS OF LEARNING (APPENDIX B)

The Applications of Learning are taken directly from the Illinois State Board of Education website and are specific to the science curriculum (*ISBE Applications of Learning*, nd.). The Applications of Learning document, while specific to the state of Illinois, addresses universal requirements in learning and assessment that we believe should be present in every classroom. Therefore, although our rubrics are designed specifically around this Illinois State Board of Education document, they are suitable for any classroom. We have also included a list of which national standards are addressed at the beginning of each chapter for your convenience.

The Applications of Learning focus on the following five main categories:

1. Solving Problems
2. Communicating
3. Using Technology
4. Making Connections
5. Working in Teams

Each of the main categories is broken down into smaller, more specific categories. This Applications of Learning rubric was used to develop all of the rubrics I use in my classes to assess student learning. The rubrics that are included in the chapters for each assessment are based on the Applications of Learning rubric, as are the numbering/lettering systems shown within the rubrics.

## LAB REPORT STYLE GUIDE (APPENDIX C)

The lab report is organized in the following outline format:

1. Introduction
   a. Background Information
   b. Purpose
   c. Hypothesis
   d. Procedure
   e. Materials Used
2. Data
   a. Data Tables From Observations
3. Analysis
   a. Graphs of Data
   b. Calculations
      i. Data Calculations
      ii. Percent Error or Percent Difference Calculations
4. Conclusion
5. Discussion Questions

This outline format is the model that students will use to report their findings for each of the five performance assessments throughout the year. The rubrics give the students the specific details about what needs to be included in each section, but the order in which their findings are presented always follows this lab outline.

## FORENSIC TAGS (APPENDIX D)

The forensics tags are used to label any evidence for each of the assessments. The tag always tells students a description of the item, the location of the item, and then leaves space for any additional information that might need to be included about the item.

## SAMPLE INQUIRY-BASED LAB (APPENDIX E)

In this climate change-focused, inquiry-based lab, solving the murder of Dr. BrINClHOF will prepare your students for the performance assessments given throughout the course. It is a great way to review material that students may have forgotten between their first year of chemistry and their second.

## REFERENCE

ISBE. *Applications of learning.* n.d. Available online at *www. isbe.net/ils/science/standards.htm*

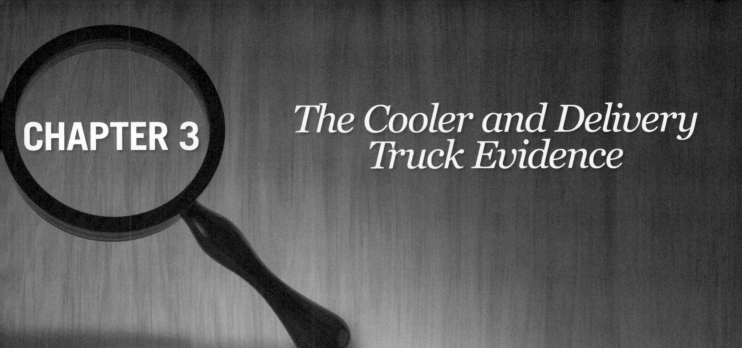

# CHAPTER 3

# The Cooler and Delivery Truck Evidence

## CHEMISTRY CONTENT

- Density
- Data interpretation
- Dimensional analysis (unit conversions)
- Gas laws
- Kinetic molecular theory
- Surface tension

## NATIONAL SCIENCE EDUCATION STANDARDS ADDRESSED

Content Standard A: Science as Inquiry
Content Standard B: Physical Science
Content Standard G: History and Nature of Science

## CASE INFORMATION

Based on your students' knowledge of chemistry, local police have asked for their help in solving a local missing-persons case. The victim in this case is Kirsten K. Your students will try to determine which of the suspects is most likely responsible for her disappearance based on the evidence provided by the police and analyzed by the students. The included suspect file provides additional evidence and the relationships of the suspects to one another. Suspects in this case include:

1. Harold M., a local plumber
2. Gladys V., a retired pharmacist and Lake House owner
3. Elizabeth G., a neighbor of the victim and local business owner
4. Larry J., the victim's husband

In the first part of this performance assessment, your students will analyze samples from a recycling plant to determine where police should begin their search for the victim. In the second part, your students will analyze data from an airbag deployment to determine whether the delivery truck driven by the victim prior to her disappearance can be extracted from the lake so that further evidence can be recovered.

### Part I: The Cooler Evidence

In Part I of this performance assessment, students learn that Kirsten K. has been reported missing and is believed to have been murdered, although this has not yet been confirmed. However, police are not sure where to start looking for the body. Police have narrowed their search down to three local bodies of water but need the students' help to determine in which body of water they should start their search. Choosing the bodies of water is up to the discretion of the teacher.

The students find out that the police received a call from a local recycling plant of a suspicious person who came into the plant with a blue cooler that had a bullet hole in it. The person of interest was also carrying a large chain. Police believe the suspect may have tried to destroy evidence by sending the cooler through the recycling plant. Students then receive baggies of recycled pieces from the plant. The recycled sample has blue, yellow, and white pieces of small plastic, all with different densities. According to the police report, the blue pieces are believed to be part of the cooler. The recycled sample baggies are labeled with a forensics tag, as seen in Figure 3.1 (for a full sheet of forensic tags, see Appendix D).

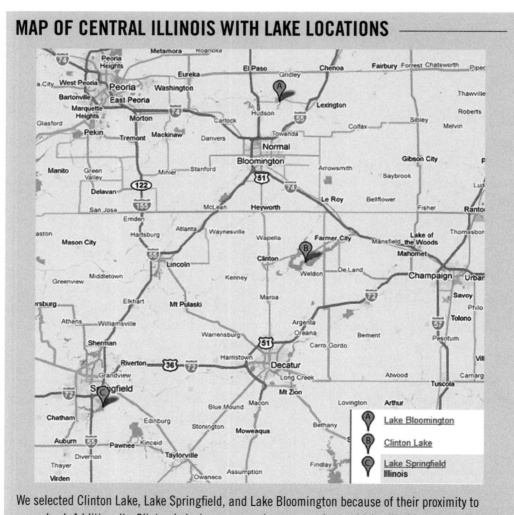

**MAP OF CENTRAL ILLINOIS WITH LAKE LOCATIONS**

A — Lake Bloomington
B — Clinton Lake
C — Lake Springfield
Illinois

We selected Clinton Lake, Lake Springfield, and Lake Bloomington because of their proximity to our school. Additionally, Clinton Lake is near a nuclear power plant, which will aid us in analyzing evidence in the Nuclear Radiation assessment presented in Chapter 5.

## FIGURE 3.1 ———————————

**FORENSIC TAG**

### Forensics Evidence Tag

**Description of item:**
Recycled cooler sample

**Location of collection:**
Local recycling plant

**Additional Information:**
Other recycled products may be included in
sample

location. Given the density ranges of the bodies of water and a variety of liquids with varying densities, the students design their own experiment to determine the density of the cooler and, therefore, in which body of water the cooler pieces will float.

In this activity, many methods can be used to solve this piece of the forensic puzzle, and students may use any materials they request, including the cups and spoons that come with the kit, as well as their lab drawer filled with standard chemistry equipment. You are likely to get a variety of experimental procedures from your students. In fact, each lab group may have a slightly different experiment or method, which is one of the benefits of inquiry-based lab activities such as this. Some students only test the blue pieces out of the sample because the cooler was blue; whereas, other students test the whole sample. Some measure or count to make sure each sample has the same number of pieces, while others don't measure or count anything. The only concept that I make sure to remind them of is "surface tension," which we studied in the previous unit. Sometimes the pieces are so small they are not able to overcome surface tension, making it appear as if the cooler pieces float at various densities. It is important that

Students learn that the police believe one of the suspects tried to dispose of the body by stuffing it into a cooler and sinking it in one of the three bodies of water. The police believe the suspect was unable to sink the cooler and so tried to dispose of the body elsewhere and recycle the cooler to get rid of the evidence. Therefore, if the students can determine the body of water in which the cooler pieces float, the police can begin searching for the victim near that

We wanted the pieces of the cooler to float in the Clinton Lake sample because we knew we wanted to use the nuclear power plant later. Whatever you decide, just make sure that the body of water you select as the starting point for the police search has the same density range as the pieces of plastic you choose to represent the cooler.

the cooler pieces float only in the density range of the body of water you wish to use as your investigation starting point.

In this assessment, students will also do a series of calculations to determine the likelihood of sinking the cooler using various methods. They will calculate whether or not the body would fit in the cooler, if the cooler would sink with the body in it, if the cooler would sink with a chain around it, and if the cooler would sink with a bullet hole in it that allowed it to fill with water. In all cases, the students' calculations support the fact that the blue cooler would not sink in any of the given situations, which leads them to the reason why the suspect would recycle the cooler instead of throwing it to the bottom of the lake. This also leads police to believe that the body of Kirsten K. still needs to be found and that they should start looking at the location identified by the students based on the recycled cooler data.

## Part II: The Delivery Truck Evidence

In Part II of the assessment, police have discovered a wedding cake delivery truck with a deployed airbag found in the lake matching the evidence from Part I. The delivery truck is believed to have been the truck that Kirsten K. was using to deliver wedding cakes on the night of her disappearance. Police need to know if they can extract the delivery truck from the lake without the volume of the airbag exceeding its maximum volume of 65 L, so that the deployed airbag stays intact and further evidence can be gathered from inside the delivery truck. Police have taken the temperature and pressure measurements at various depths in the lake, which will allow students to calculate how the volume of the airbag will change as the delivery truck is brought up to the surface of the lake. In addition, students will graph the evidence to show the various trends relating to gas laws. Students are expected to recognize if the trend shown in their graph is a direct or an indirect relationship. Students should find that the airbag will not explode, so further evidence can be gathered from the delivery truck. In this part of the assessment, students are also asked to calculate the number of moles of gas that will fill the airbag at a given temperature, maximum volume, and pressure. They will also need to explain how the number of moles of gas does not change as the delivery truck with the deployed airbag is brought to the surface of the lake. Based on the cooler and delivery truck evidence, students are allowed to create whatever scenario fits within their conclusions. The importance of the evidence collected from this performance assessment in the overall case will depend on other evidence collected through the other four performance assessments, especially the chemical evidence in assessment #2 (see Chapter 4: The Chemical Evidence).

In the remaining pages of this chapter, you will find a teacher guide, student handout, suspect file, student lab report example, and grading rubric for Performance Assessment 1: The Cooler and Delivery Truck Evidence. More information about how to use the grading rubric for this and future performance assessments can be found in Appendix B.

# Teacher Guide:
## *The Cooler and Delivery Truck Evidence*

**Time:** 4–5 days
**Grades:** 11 and 12 (second-year chemistry)

## OBJECTIVES

1. Students will solve a forensics case using their knowledge of chemistry (for performance assessment #1 this includes density, data interpretation, dimensional analysis, gas laws, kinetic molecular theory, and surface tension).
2. Students will assemble their evidence in the format of a lab report.
3. Students will answer the following questions:

### *Part I*

1. What is the density range of the blue cooler pieces?
2. In which lake should police begin their search for the body?
3. Would the body fit inside the cooler?
4. Would the cooler have been able to float with the body in it, plus a chain wrapped around it?
5. Would the cooler float after water filled it through a bullet hole?

### *Part II*

1. According to volume data, explain why the police should be able to still get evidence from the delivery truck after retrieving the truck from the lake?
2. Describe the pressure verses volume graph. Use the words *direct* or *inverse* in your description of the relationship, along with data from the graph, in your answer to describe which gas law this graph represents.
3. Describe the volume verses temperature graph. Use the words *direct* or *inverse* in your description of the relationship, along with data from the graph, in your answer to describe which gas law this graph represents.
4. Using the ideas supporting the kinetic molecular theory, explain why the number of moles of gas in the deployed airbag would stay the same throughout the volume calculations.

## PREPARATION

### *Part I*

Students will need a variety of liquids with varying densities in order to determine the density range for the **blue** cooler pieces from the recycled sample. The recycled sample consists of polystyrene (blue pieces), nylon (yellow pieces), acrylic (white pieces), and polypropylene (clear pieces), which have density ranges of 1.05–1.07 g/ml, 1.15 g/ml, 1.15–1.20 g/ml, and 0.90–0.91 g/ml respectively. Make sure the density range of the cooler matches the density range of the lake near which the investigation will take place.

*Part II*

No setup required for this part.

## THE LAB

### Part I

Students write their own hypothesis, design their own procedure, and create their own data table. The work that they do will be assembled in a lab report as part of their evidence file (to be maintained throughout the year).

### Part II

Students will be graphing and analyzing data collected by the police about volume, pressure, and temperature and calculate using the ideal gas law.

## QUESTION GUIDELINES

For calculations, formulas, and work, see the student example at the end of the chapter.

### Part I

1.  The blue cooler pieces should have a density range of 1.05–1.07 g/ml (NOTE: one likely source of error in this range would be the result of surface tension of the liquids when determining the density range of the plastic pieces).
2.  Clinton lake (of the three lake density ranges, the cooler pieces should float in this range ONLY).
3.  Yes, the body of Kirsten K. would fit in the cooler.
4.  Yes, the cooler would only be partially submerged because the height of the water displaced is not greater than the height of the cooler.
5.  Yes, it will still float even if it was filled with water so the suspect(s) had to dispose of the cooler by recycling it.

### Part II

1.  The airbag volume will not go above the maximum 65 L as calculated for each of the various depths. The maximum volume of the airbag only gets to 63.8 L at the surface as the delivery truck is extracted from Clinton Lake, so evidence should still be able to be collected from inside the delivery truck.
2.  The pressure verses volume graph shows an indirect relationship. The volume of the airbag at the bottom of the lake is 27.1 L and the pressure is 2.24 atm, but as the volume increases to 64 L as the truck gets closer to the surface of the lake, the pressure decreases to 1.01 atm. This shows the relationship in Boyle's Law.
3.  The volume verses temperature graph shows a direct relationship. The volume of the airbag is 27.1 L and the temperature is 5°C, but as the temperature is increased to 22°C near the surface of the lake, the volume of the airbag increases to 63.8 L. This shows the relationship in Charles' Law.
4.  As long as the airbag stays closed and is not punctured with holes at all as the delivery truck is being extracted from the lake, the number of moles of gas will stay the same inside the airbag. According to the kinetic molecular theory, the gas molecules inside the airbag will increase in movement as the temperature of the molecules is increased as the truck is brought to the surface. This would also account for the airbag's change in volume; the greater number of collisions of the molecules inside the airbag is caused by the increase in their movement as the temperature increases.

# MATERIALS

## *Part I*

- Recycled sample
  - Mixture Separation Challenge (a kit from Educational Innovations)
  - *www.teachersource.com/Density/DensityKits/MixtureSeparationChallenge.aspx*
- Various liquid samples with varying densities. Some examples include: water (1.000 g/ml), salt water (1.03–1.05 g/ml), 95% EtOH (0.789 g/ml), 90% isopropyl alcohol (0.786 g/ml), canola oil (0.912–0.924 g/ml)
- Forensic tags (included in Appendix D)
- Suspect File A
- Additional supplies may include: spoons, plastic cups, beakers, graduated cylinders, tweezers

## *Part II*

- Graph Paper (included in the assessment handout)

Name:_____ Class:_____ Date:_____

# The Case of Kirsten K.:
## *The Cooler and Delivery Truck Evidence*

## PART I: THE COOLER EVIDENCE

### *Case Background*

On September 4, Kirsten K. went missing from the Bloomington-Normal area. A missing person's report was filed by her husband, Larry J., and the police are still investigating. No sign of the body has been found yet, but police are currently investigating a lead and have narrowed their search down to four suspects. Police were informed that one of the suspects was seen taking a cooler to a recycling plant after allegedly dumping the body. When questioned, the manager of the recycling plant remembered a blue cooler being brought in sometime early in the week of September 7. He remembers it for two reasons:

1.  It had what looked like a bullet hole in it, and he remembers thinking "it wouldn't work very well as a cooler with a hole in it."
2.  The suspect was carrying a chain in the other hand when dropping off the cooler.

Police confiscated the recycled sample, which included pieces of the cooler and other items that were recycled with it. The recycled sample is currently en route to the CSI (Crime Scene Investigation) lab at the local police station. Police believe the suspect(s) stored the missing body inside of the cooler at one point in an attempt to dispose of the body in one of the following lakes: Lake Bloomington, Clinton Lake, or Lake Springfield. Police believe that the suspect(s) tried to recycle the evidence after failing to sink the cooler in one of these bodies of water.

### *Background Information on the Lakes*

*Lake Bloomington*—located just north of Bloomington, Illinois, this lake has a surface area of 635 acres and an average density of 0.98 g/ml. The smaller size of this lake allows for the water to change temperature more rapidly than the other lakes in the area. Therefore, the water in Lake Bloomington is, on average, warmer than in the other lakes. This means that less gas is dissolved in the water, making it *slightly* less dense than the average density of water.

*Clinton Lake*—located approximately 30 miles south of Bloomington, Illinois, this lake has a surface area of 4,900 acres and an average density of 1.05 g/ml. The larger size of this lake means that the water temperature does not change as rapidly as smaller lakes. Therefore, the water in Clinton Lake is, on average, cooler than in the other lakes. This allows for more gas to be dissolved in the water, making it denser than the average density of water.

*Lake Springfield*—located approximately 50 miles south of Bloomington, Illinois, this lake has a surface area of 4,234 acres and an average density of 1.01 g/ml. The lake is of average size and of average temperature.

## Purpose

Your investigation should help police determine answers to the following three questions:

1. What is the density range of the cooler in which the suspect(s) tried to store the missing body?
2. In which body of water should police start looking for the body?
3. Would the suspect(s) have been successful in trying to dispose of the body, by sinking it in the cooler using the methods described?

## Hypothesis

In which scenarios (e.g., bullet holes, chains, filling with water) would the suspect(s) have been successful or unsuccessful in sinking the cooler? Address all scenarios in your hypothesis.

_____

_____

_____

_____

_____

## Procedure

Write out your experimental procedure (numbered list of steps) below. Be specific!

_____

_____

_____

_____

_____

_____

## Materials

- Various liquids of varying densities
- Recycled sample
- Small dishes
- Spoons

## Data

Construct a data table or tables to collect data as described in the procedure.

## ANALYSIS: CALCULATIONS

There are thee key questions that the police must address in order to verify or refute the evidence from the cooler:

1.  Would the body have actually fit inside the cooler?
2.  Would the cooler have even been able to float with the body inside?
3.  Would the cooler have floated with a bullet hole in it that would have allowed water to fill the cooler?

Answer the questions below, which will help to answer these three key questions. Address these three questions in your conclusion and support them with the calculations below.

1.  The igloo cooler that was used in this case was believed to have had the labeled capacity of 162 qts. Kirsten K.'s body had a volume of approximately 59.5 L (0.95 L = 1 qt.). Would the body have even fit in the cooler? Show work to support your answer.

2.  The cooler was believed to have had dimensions of 104 cm long, 45.7 cm wide, and 53.3 cm deep. If the cooler sinks one cm, calculate the volume of water it displaces.

3.  The density of lake water where you determined police should start their investigation is _____ g/cm$^3$. Calculate the mass in kilograms of the lake water displaced by the volume you calculated in question #2 (1,000 g = 1 kg).

4.  Kirsten K.'s body weighed 128 lbs. The empty cooler has a mass of 13.6 kg, and the chain that police believed the suspect wrapped around the cooler to try to make it sink, has a mass of 13.6 kg as well. Calculate the total mass of the body, the cooler, and the chain. Using your calculation from question #3, how many centimeters will the cooler holding the body and wrapped in chains sink? Will the cooler be completely submerged below the surface of the water? (1 kg = 2.21 lbs)

5.  Now let's determine if the cooler will still float if you shoot a hole in it and allow water to enter. Let's consider the extreme case in which water fills the entire cooler (which it won't). The inside dimensions of the cooler are 35.5 cm by 94.0 cm by 43.2 cm deep. Calculate the inside volume of the cooler in liters. (1 ml = 1 cm$^3$)

6. Calculate the mass of lake/creek water that would completely fill the cooler. Remember to use the density of lake/creek water that you chose in the cooler evidence.

7. Calculate the total mass of the cooler, chain, and lake/creek water. How many centimeters will the cooler sink? Will it be completely submerged if it is full of lake/creek water?

## Conclusion

In which body of water should the police start their investigation and what specific data supports this? Be sure to refer back to your hypothesis.

## Discussion

1. Describe the likelihood of the body being able to fit inside the cooler. Use calculations to support your answer.

2. Describe the ways in which the suspects tried to dispose of the cooler. Were they successful? Support your statement with evidence.

3. Describe what effect the bullet hole would have had on the ability of the coolor to sink in the lake.

Part I—The Cooler Evidence: adapted from "Murder She Floats," by Robert Mentzner, ChemMatters, Dec. 2002, pp. 17–19. Copyright 2002 American Chemical Society.

## PART II: THE DELIVERY TRUCK EVIDENCE

### Background Information About Airbags

A sensor in front of a car detects sudden deceleration and sends a signal to a cylinder containing a mixture of chemicals. In the cylinder, an igniter goes off, starting a series of chemical reactions that release a large volume of nitrogen gas. The bag literally bursts from its storage site at up to 200 mph. When the airbag deploys, the maximum volume it can hold is 65 L. The gas fills the airbag, and the passenger hits the soft bag instead of the steering wheel or dashboard. A second later the gas quickly dissipates through tiny holes in the bag, thus deflating the bag so the person can move. The bag has to inflate in less than a tenth of a second, and it has to inflate with exactly the right amount of gas. If it under-inflates, it would not provide enough protection; if it over-inflates, it might rupture or cause an explosion.

The first reaction set off by the igniter is the decomposition of sodium azide into sodium metal and nitrogen gas.

$$2NaN_3 \rightarrow 2Na + 3N_2$$

By itself, this reaction cannot fill the airbag fast enough, and the sodium metal that is produced is dangerously reactive. To solve these problems, engineers included potassium nitrate in the mixture of reactants. The potassium nitrate reacts with the sodium produced in the first reaction, releasing even more nitrogen gas.

$$10Na + 2KNO_3 \rightarrow K_2O + 5Na_2O + N_2$$

The heat released by this reaction raises the temperature of the gaseous product, helping the bag inflate even faster. The heat causes all the solid reaction products to fuse together with $SiO_2$, powdered sand, which is also part of the reaction mixture.

### Background Information About the Case

Police have started searching Clinton Lake, as you suggested, looking for evidence regarding the missing person's report they received for Kirsten K. Police have found an abandoned delivery truck at the bottom of the lake, which may hold evidence that could lead to finding the person(s) responsible for the kidnapping of Kirsten K. The airbag has been deployed, but there was a malfunction and the airbag remained inflated even after entering the lake. Police want to make sure the airbag will not explode as they lift the truck up from the bottom of the lake to the surface in order to preserve all possible evidence in the delivery truck that has not yet been destroyed. They have asked you to help collect evidence and double check some of the data they have already taken.

### Purpose

To determine if the vehicle can be safely removed from the lake without the airbag exploding.

### Hypothesis

Looking at the data provided by the police about depth, temperature, and pressure of the lake, predict what will happen to the volume of the airbag as the truck is removed from the bottom of Clinton Lake. Consider the Pressure (P), Temperature (T), and Volume (V) relationships as well when giving your prediction.

### Data

Table 1 shows the lake data from the police including depths, temperatures, and pressures to help you determine the volume of the airbag at various depths.

### Analysis: Graphing

Before you arrived at the scene, police started to collect data about the temperature, pressure, and volume to try to gain more information about the abandoned vehicle.

## TABLE 1

**CLINTON LAKE DATA MEASUREMENTS FROM POLICE**

| DEPTH (FEET) | TEMPERATURE (°C) | PRESSURE | CALCULATED VOLUME (L) |
|---|---|---|---|
| 40 | 5 | 2.24 atm | |
| 30 | 10 | 1520 mmHg | |
| 20 | 15 | 1140 mmHg | |
| 10 | 20 | 1.07 atm | |
| 0 | 22 | 1.01 atm | |

## GRAPH #1

**PRESSURE VS. VOLUME**

Graph the pressure from the lake verses the volume to show the relationship between the two variables.

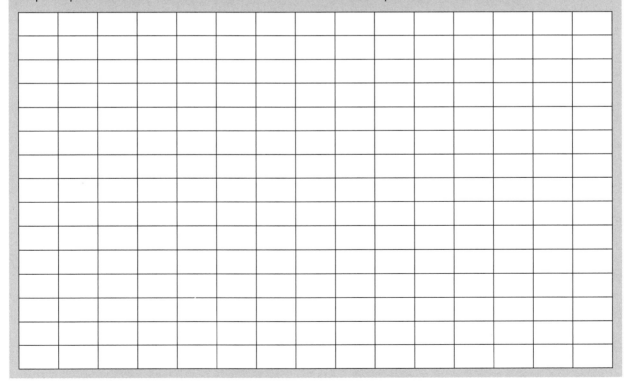

## GRAPH #2

**VOLUME VS. TEMPERATURE**

Graph the volume that you calculated for each of the various temperatures in the lake to show the relationship between the two variables. (***You will not be able to create this graph until after you do the Analysis-Calculations section of the assessment.)

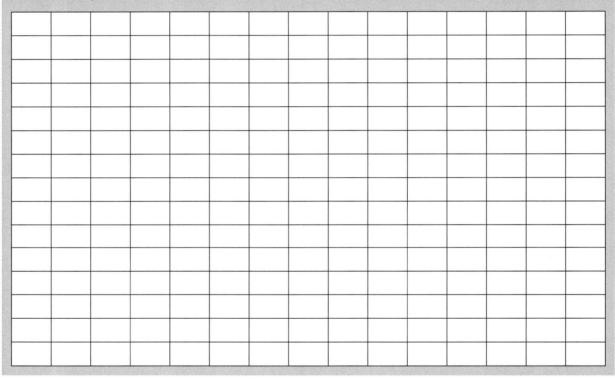

### *Analysis: Calculations*

You have been hired by the police as a chemical engineer responsible for investigating the abandoned vehicle found with a deployed air bag. For police to gain insight into the case, they need you to calculate if the delivery truck can be safely removed from the lake without the airbag expanding too much, bursting, and destroying evidence.

1. Calculate the number of moles of gas in the airbag at maximum volume, 65 liters, at room temperature, 25°C, and at 1 atmosphere (atm) of pressure.

2. Calculate the volume at the various depths given by the police to determine if the airbag will expand to a volume greate enough to make it explode.

| DEPTH (FT) | VOLUME CALCULATIONS USING IDEAL GAS LAW |
|---|---|
| 40 | |
| 30 | |
| 20 | |
| 10 | |
| 0 | |

## Conclusion

Explain to the police whether or not they will be able to gather evidence from the delivery truck and why, based on your calculations.

## Discussion Questions

1. According to volume data, will the police be able to retrieve evidence from the delivery truck after raising the truck from the lake? Explain.

_____
_____
_____
_____
_____
_____

2. Describe the pressure verses volume graph. Use the words *direct* or *inverse* in your description of the relationship, along with data from the graph, in your answer to describe which gas law this graph represents.

_____
_____
_____
_____
_____
_____

3. Describe the volume verses temperature graph. Use the words *direct* or *inverse* in your description of the relationship, along with data from the graph, in your answer to describe which gas law this graph represents.

_____
_____
_____
_____
_____

4. Using the ideas supporting the kinetic molecular theory, explain why the number of moles of gas in the deployed airbag would stay the same throughout the volume calculations.

_____
_____
_____
_____
_____
_____

# SUSPECT FILE A

### Victim: Kirsten K.

Occupation: Nurse

Residence: Normal, IL.

### Suspect #1: Harold M.

Occupation: Plumber

Residence: Clinton, IL. (just off Highway 10)

### Suspect #2: Gladys V.

Occupation: Retired pharmacist

Residence: Bloomington, IL (Owns a lake house on
Clinton Lake)

### Suspect #3: Elizabeth G.

Occupation: Owner of a wedding cake design/
catering business

Residence: Normal, IL (neighbor to the victim and
her husband)

### Suspect #4: Larry J.

Occupation: Investment banker

Residence: Normal, IL (husband of the victim)

Name:_____ Class:_____ Date:_____

# Student Lab Report Example:
## *The Cooler and Delivery Truck Evidence*

## I. INTRODUCTION

### (A) Background Information

The cooler was found in the recycling plant with a bullet hole in it. The fact that the cooler was taken to the factory by a person carrying a chain helps solidify that the chain, cooler, and bullet hole can be submitted into evidence. The victim, Kirsten K., was disposed of in Lake Bloomington, Clinton Lake, or Lake Springfield. By using the information provided by the police, it will be possible to determine if the truck found had anything to do with Kirsten K.'s murder as long as the airbag stays intact as they extract the delivery truck from the lake.

### (B) Purpose

The purpose is to discover where the crime scene is located for the kidnapping of Kirsten K. and to calculate if the suspect(s) could have sunk the victim in a cooler into the lake. It also needs to be determined if the sunken delivery truck can be removed from the lake without it bursting as it rises to the surface, so evidence can be used from the truck to find the prime suspects at this point in the investigation.

### (C) Hypothesis

If there was a body in the cooler, a bullet hole in it, and a chain wrapped around it, then it will still float and the suspect will have to dispose of the cooler differently which is why the cooler had to be recycled.

If the police are able to remove the truck from the lake without the volume going over 65 L, then the evidence from the sunken delivery truck will be able to safely be retrieved.

### (D) Procedure

1. Pour the various liquids into the cups provided using the same amount of liquid in each cup.
2. Place the same number of blue pieces in each cup of liquid.
3. Use a spoon to push down on the blue pieces to make sure they are not floating because of surface tension.

4. Record whether or not the blue pieces sink or float in the liquid.
    a. If cooler sample sinks, then the density of the blue cooler pieces is greater than the density of that liquid.
    b. If the cooler sample floats, then the density of the blue cooler pieces is less than the density of that liquid.

## (E) Materials

Various known liquids with different densities
Recycled sample containing blue cooler pieces
Small dishes
Spoons

## II. DATA

### Part 1: The Cooler Evidence
### TABLE 1:

**RECYCLED COOLER AND LAKE SAMPLES**

| LIQUID | DENSITY (G/ML) | SINKS | FLOATS |
|---|---|---|---|
| Water | 1.00 | Yes | No |
| Salt | 1.05 | No | Yes |
| Ethanol | 0.79 | Yes | No |
| Mineral Oil | 0.80 | Yes | No |
| Vinegar | 1.01 | Yes | No |

### Part II: The Delivery Truck Evidence
### TABLE 2:

**CALCULATED VOLUME OF AIRBAG FROM THE SUNKEN DELIVERY TRUCK**

| DEPTH (FEET) | TEMPERATURE (⁰C) | PRESSURE (ATM) | CALCULATED VOLUME (LITERS) |
|---|---|---|---|
| 40 | 5 | 2.24 atm | 27.1 |
| 30 | 10 | $1.520 \text{ mmHg} \times \frac{1 \text{ atm}}{760 \text{ atm}} = 1.17 \text{ atm}$ | 30.9 |
| 20 | 15 | $1140 \text{ mmHg} \times \frac{1 \text{ atm}}{760 \text{ atm}} = 1.10 \text{ atm}$ | 57.2 |
| 10 | 20 | 1.07 atm | 59.8 |
| 0 | 22 | 1.01 atm | 63.8 |

# III. ANALYSIS: CALCULATIONS

**GRAPH 1: PRESSURE VS. VOLUME**

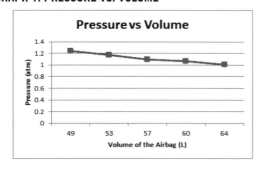

**GRAPH 2: VOLUME VS. TEMPERATURE**

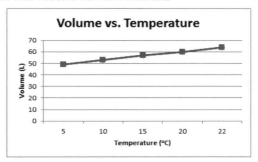

## Part I: The Cooler Evidence

1.  $59.5 \text{ L} \times \dfrac{1.057 \text{ qts}}{\text{L}} = 62.9 \text{ qts}$

    >162 qts = body does not fit
    <162 qts = body does fit
    62.9 qts < 162 qts = yes, body will fit inside the cooler

2.  1 ml = 1 cm³
    104 cm x 45.7 cm x 1 cm = 4,752.8 cm³ of water displaced if cooler sinks 1 cm

3.  $4{,}752.8 \text{ cm}^3 \times \dfrac{1.05 \text{ g}}{1 \text{ cm}^3} = 4990.4 \text{ g} \times \dfrac{1000 \text{ g}}{1 \text{ kg}} = 4.9904 \text{ kg}$

    OR

    Density = mass/volume      1.05 g/cm³ = mass/4,752.8 cm³
                               Mass = 4,990.4 g

4.  128 lbs x 1 kg = 58.2 kg + 13.6 kg + 13.6 kg = 85.4 kg
                      (body)     (cooler)    (chain)

    $\dfrac{4.9904 \text{ kg}}{1 \text{ cm}} = \dfrac{85.4 \text{ kg}}{x \text{ cm}}$

    x = 17.1 cm → no, not completely submerged because it's below the cooler height
                   of 53.5 cm

5.  35.5 cm x 94.0 cm x 43.2 cm = 144158.4 ml x $\dfrac{1 \text{ L}}{1000 \text{ml}}$ = 144 L

    Volume = length x width x height
    1 cm³ = 1 ml = 0.001 L

6.  $144 \text{ L} \times \dfrac{1000 \text{ ml}}{1 \text{ L}} \times \dfrac{1 \text{ cm}^3}{1 \text{ ml}} \times \dfrac{1.05 \text{ g}}{1 \text{ cm}^3} = 151,200 \text{ g} \times \dfrac{1 \text{ kg}}{1000 \text{ g}} = 151 \text{ kg}$

7.  $\underset{\text{(salt water)}}{151 \text{ kg}} + \underset{\text{(chain)}}{13.6 \text{ kg}} + \underset{\text{(cooler)}}{13.6 \text{ kg}} = 178 \text{ kg}$

$$\dfrac{4.9904 \text{ kg}}{1 \text{ cm}} = \dfrac{178 \text{ kg}}{x \text{ cm}}$$

$x = 35.7 \text{ cm} \rightarrow$ no, not completely submerged because it's below the cooler height of 53.5 cm

## PART II: THE DELIVERY TRUCK EVIDENCE

1.  Ideal Gas Law

    $P = 1 \text{ atm}$

    $V = 65 \text{ L}$

    $R = 0.0821 \text{ L-atm/mole-K}$

    $T = 25^{\circ}\text{C} + 273 = 298\text{K}$

    $P V = n R T$

    $(1) \times (65) = n \times (0.0821) \times (298)$

    $65 = n \times (24.4658)$

    $n = 2.66 \text{ moles}$

2.

| CALCULATIONS FOR THE VOLUME OF THE AIRBAG AT VARIOUS DEPTHS | |
|---|---|
| **DEPTH (FEET)** | **VOLUME CALCULATIONS USING IDEAL GAS LAW** |
| 40 | $P V = n R T$<br>$(2.24) \times (V) = (2.66) \times (0.0821) \times (278)$<br>$2.24 V = (60.7)$<br>$V = 27.1 L$ |
| 30 | $P V = n R T$<br>$(2.0) \times (V) = (2.66) \times (0.0821) \times (283)$<br>$2.0 V = (61.8)$<br>$V = 30.9 L$ |
| 20 | $P V = n R T$<br>$(1.5) \times (V) = (2.66) \times (0.0821) \times (288)$<br>$1.5 V = (41.9)$<br>$V = 57.2 L$ |
| 10 | $P V = n R T$<br>$(1.07) \times (V) = (2.66) \times (0.0821) \times (293)$<br>$1.07 V = (64.0)$<br>$V = 59.8 L$ |
| 0 | $P V = n R T$<br>$(1.01) \times (V) = (2.66) \times (0.0821) \times (295)$<br>$1.01 V = (64.4)$<br>$V = 63.8 L$ |

## IV. CONCLUSION

The purpose of the experiments was to be able to find the location of the crime scene where the kidnapping of Kirsten K. took place, determine if the body was able to be disposed of inside the cooler using the various options, and check to see if the delivery truck could be safely removed from the lake without the deployed airbag exploding. The hypothesis was supported for Part I: The Cooler Evidence because the suspect(s) were not successful in trying to sink the cooler with the body in it, with a chain wrapped around it, or shooting a bullet hole it to allow the cooler to fill with water. The hypothesis for Part II: The Delivery Truck Evidence was also supported because the airbag did not increase above 65 Liters in volume so it will not explode when police remove it from the bottom of the lake, so evidence will be able to be extracted from the airbag of the truck.

    The data collected from the density gradient experiment proves that Kirsten K.'s body was disposed of in the Clinton Lake because the blue recycled cooler pieces did not float in the salt water only. The salt water had a density of 1.05 g/ml and the vinegar had the next highest density of 1.01 g/ml. The recycled blue cooler pieces did not float in the vinegar, so this puts the density of the cooler pieces between a 1.01 g/ml and 1.05 g/ml range in density. The only lake that the cooler would have floated in would have been Clinton Lake because it has a density of 1.05 g/ml. The density of Lake Springfield (1.01 g/ml) would have matched the density of the vinegar that was tested where the blue cooler pieces sank. So if the suspect(s) were trying to sink the cooler in Lake Bloomington or Lake Springfield, they would have been successful and wouldn't have had to recycle the cooler to get rid of the evidence. The calculations for the various situations create additional support for the suspect(s) not being successful in sinking the cooler using other methods, such as wrapping chain around it or shooting a hole in it to fill it with water. According to the calculations in numbers four and five specifically, even if the cooler had a hole in it, the cooler with the body in it would have still floated.

The police were also able to successfully remove the delivery truck from the lake without exploding the airbag, so additional evidence will be able to be retrieved from the truck to determine the lead suspect(s) at this point in the investigation. According to the calculations, the volume of the airbag will only get to 63.8 L and the maximum capacity of the airbag is 65 L, so the police should be able to remove the truck with the deployed airbag exploding and compromising important evidence in the truck.

The two most likely suspects for Kirsten K.'s murder are Harold M. and Gladys V. They are the best suspects because they both have houses in Clinton and live in the area and would be most familiar with Clinton Lake. Harold M. may be more likely than Gladys V. to be able to maneuver the victim and cooler to try to sink it. If Gladys V. were working alone, it would be highly unlikely that she would be able to move the cooler and chains to wrap it by herself. But since she is a retired pharmacist she may have access to drugs to kidnap the victim. But again, she is most likely not working alone since she may not have the strength required to be able to force Kirsten K. to be taken from one location to another.

## V. DISCUSSION

### Part I: The Cooler Evidence

1. Describe the likelihood of the body being able to fit inside the cooler. Use calculations to support your answer.

   The body would have fit in the cooler because according to calculation #1, the cooler can hold 162 quarts and Kirsten's body only takes up 62.9 quarts of space.

2. Describe the ways in which the suspects tried to dispose of the cooler. Were they successful? Support your statement with evidence.

   The cooler would have still floated even with the weight of Kirsten K.'s body inside of it. In calculation #2, the cooler with a mass of 4.872 kg would displace 4,753.8 cm³ of water if it sank 1 cm. But with the mass of the body inside the cooler and a chain around it, plus the mass of the cooler itself, it would have only sank 17.5 cm which is not higher than the height of the cooler, which is 53.3 cm (as stated in calculation #2).

3. Describe what effect the bullet hole would have had on the ability of the coolor to sink in the lake.

*After the suspects tried to sink the cooler with the body in it and were not successful, they now had to try to dispose of the cooler separately from the victim's body. The suspects would not have been successful trying to fill the cooler with water as it was in the lake either. With the mass of the cooler, the mass of the chain, and the mass of the water inside the cooler, the total mass of the cooler would be 175 kg. According to calculation #7, the cooler would only sink 35.7 cm, so it is not completely submerged because it does not cover the 53.5 cm height of the cooler, so some of the cooler would still be able to be seen at the top of the lake.*

## Part II: The Delivery Truck Evidence

1. According to volume data, will the police be able to retrieve evidence from the delivery truck after raising the truck from the lake?

*The maximum capacity for the volume of the airbag is 65 L, so if the volume of the airbag does not increase above the 65 L limit as the police are extracting the delivery truck from the lake, then the deployed airbag will not explode and compromise evidence. According to the calculation for volume at a depth of 0 feet (so right at the surface of the lake), the volume of the airbag was 63.8 L, which is not above the maximum capacity, so the airbag will stay intact.*

2. Describe the pressure verses volume graph. Use the words *direct* or *inverse* in your description of the relationship, along with data from the graph, in your answer to describe which gas law this graph represents.

*The pressure verses volume graph shows an indirect relationship, because the two variables in the graph do the opposite thing. According to the graph, as the pressure at the various depths in the lake decreases as the delivery truck is removed from the lake, the volume of the airbag will increase. The volume of the airbag at the bottom of the lake is 27.1 L and the pressure is 2.24 atm, but as the volume increases to 63.8 L as the truck gets closer to the surface of the lake, the pressure decreases to 1.01 atm. This shows the relationship in Boyle's Law. The only difference here is that temperature is not held constant, but the same relationship between pressure and volume is seen as in Boyle's Law.*

3. Describe the volume verses temperature graph. Use the words *direct* or *inverse* in your description of the relationship along with data from the graph in your answer to describe which gas law this graph represents.

*The volume verses temperature graph shows a direct relationship, because the two variables in the graph do the same thing. According to the graph, as the temperature increases as the truck is brought closer to the surface, the volume of the airbag increases as well. The volume of the airbag is 27.1 L and the temperature is 5°C, but as the temperature is increased to 22°C near the surface of the lake, the volume of the airbag increases to 63.8 L. This shows the relationship in Charles' Law. The only difference is that the pressure is not held constant because the pressure changes as well as the truck goes from being on the bottom of the lake to the top, closer to the surface.*

4. Using the ideas supporting the kinetic molecular theory, explain why the number of moles of gas in the deployed airbag would stay the same throughout the volume calculations.

Once the airbag deploys, there are a certain number of moles of gas produced from the reactants inside the bag. As long as the airbag stays closed and not punctured with holes at all as the delivery truck is being extracted from the lake, the number of moles of gas will stay the same inside the airbag. According to the kinetic molecular theory, the gas molecules inside the airbag will increase in movement as the temperature of the molecules are increased as the truck is brought to the surface. This would also account for why the airbag would change in volume because of the greater number of collisions of the molecules inside the airbag because of the increase in their movement from the temperature increase.

# GRADING RUBRIC A

Name _____

Score _____ /60 _____ % Grade _____

## I. Introduction

| Application | # | wgt | Exemplary (10) | At Standard (8) | In Progress (7) | Still Emerging (6) | No Evaluation (0) |
|---|---|---|---|---|---|---|---|
| Defining Problems | 1a | ½ | Makes insightful connections between ideas or events that might not be obvious—abstract thinking evident (4 of 4)<br>□ Background Information includes highlighted information about both the cooler and delivery truck cases and the suspect files that are relevant to answering the purpose<br>□ Purpose is clearly stated and correct<br>□ A hypothesis is given for both the cooler evidence testing and the delivery truck gas laws data<br>□ Procedure supports purpose with a detailed, numerical list of steps for developing a density gradient for the cooler evidence | Makes general, logical connections between ideas or events; mostly concrete in nature (3 of 4) | Makes superficial connections between ideas; thinking might be confused or incomplete (2 of 4) | Makes incorrect or no connections between ideas (1 of 4) | No work shown for this section |

## II. Data—Part I: The Cooler Evidence

| Application | # | wgt | Exemplary (10) | At Standard (8) | In Progress (7) | Still Emerging (6) | No Evaluation (0) |
|---|---|---|---|---|---|---|---|
| Interpreting Models | 1b | ½ | Interprets visuals or models at a complex level (4 of 4)<br>□ Sufficient number of tests/trials to obtain meaningful density data for each liquid sample with the blue cooler pieces<br>□ All qualitative measurements are accurately recorded in a data table format, not just listed<br>□ Completed data table includes a relevant **title** explaining the data sets<br>□ Correct labels/units are used for the qualitative data | Interprets visuals or models at a general level (3 of 4) | Interpretation of visual or model contains errors that restrict understanding (2 of 4) | Shows fundamental errors in use and understanding of visual (1 of 4) | No work turned in for this section |

## II. Data—Part II: The Delivery Truck Evidence

| Application | # | wgt | Exemplary (10) | At Standard (8) | In Progress (7) | Still Emerging (6) | No Evaluation (0) |
|---|---|---|---|---|---|---|---|
| Interpreting Models | 1b | ½ | Interprets visuals or models at a complex level (4 of 4)<br>□ The calculated volume for each depth is shown in a data table format<br>□ All calculated measurements for converting the mmHg to atm are shown within the data table, not just listed<br>□ Completed data table includes a relevant **title** explaining the data sets<br>□ Correct labels/units are used for both the qualitative and quantitative data | Interprets visuals or models at a general level (3 of 4) | Interpretation of visual or model contains errors that restrict understanding (2 of 4) | Shows fundamental errors in use and understanding of visual (1 of 4) | No work turned in for this section |

## III. Analysis: Graph—Part II: The Delivery Truck Evidence

| Application | # | wgt | Exemplary (10) | At Standard (8) | In Progress (7) | Still Emerging (6) | No Evaluation (0) |
|---|---|---|---|---|---|---|---|
| Interpreting Models | 1b | ½ | Interprets visuals or models at a complex level (4 of 4)<br>☐ Points are plotted correctly on both of the gas law graphs and even intervals are shown on both axes of the graph<br>☐ A best fit line is correctly drawn for each of the graphs for both relationships<br>☐ Completed graphs include a relevant title explaining the data sets<br>☐ Correct labels/units are used for both the x and y-axis | Interprets visuals or models at a general level (3 of 4) | Interpretation of visuals or models contains errors that restrict understanding (2 of 4) | Shows fundamental errors in use and understanding of visuals (1 of 4) | No work turned in for this section |

## III. Analysis: Calculations—Part I: The Cooler Evidence

| Application | # | wgt | Exemplary (10) | At Standard (8) | In Progress (7) | Still Emerging (6) | No Evaluation (0) |
|---|---|---|---|---|---|---|---|
| Problem Calculations | 2a | ½ | All essential information is evident through well-organized work while justifying the solution (4 of 4)<br>☐ Calculations (#1) for proving discussion question #1 are complete, correct, and all work was shown including units for all numbers throughout calculation<br>☐ Calculations (#2-#4) for proving discussion question #2 are complete, correct, and all work was shown including units for all numbers throughout calculation<br>☐ Calculations (#5-#7) for proving discussion question #3 are complete, correct, and all work was shown including units for all numbers throughout calculation<br>☐ Significant figures are considered when writing final answers for each of the calculations | Most essential information is evident through organized work while leading to the solution (3 of 4) | Minimum information is evident through work with a solution present (2 of 4) | Work is extremely unorganized with no solution present (1 of 4) | No work shown for this section |

## III. Analysis: Calculations—Part II: The Delivery Truck Evidence

| Application | # | wgt | Exemplary (10) | At Standard (8) | In Progress (7) | Still Emerging (6) | No Evaluation (0) |
|---|---|---|---|---|---|---|---|
| Problem Calculations | 2a | ½ | All essential information is evident through well-organized work while justifying the solution (4 of 4)<br>☐ The correct equation was shown for the gas law that was used for calculating the number of moles of gas in the airbag and the volume at each of the depths<br>☐ Calculations for the number of moles of gas in the airbag are complete, correct, and all work was shown<br>☐ Calculations for the volume of the airbag at various depths are complete, correct, and all work was shown<br>☐ Units for ALL numbers were consistently used throughout the calculations in this section | Most essential information is evident through organized work while leading to the solution (3 of 4) | Minimum information is evident through work with a solution present (2 of 4) | Work is extremely unorganized with no solution present (1 of 4) | No work shown for this section |

## IV. Conclusion—Part 1: The Cooler Evidence

| Application | # | wgt | Exemplary (10) | At Standard (8) | In Progress (7) | Still Emerging (6) | No Evaluation (0) |
|---|---|---|---|---|---|---|---|
| Connecting Ideas | 1d | ½ | Makes insightful connections between ideas or events that might not be obvious—abstract thinking evident (4 of 4)<br>☐ The purpose is answered for which lake police should start looking around to find more evidence and designate a crime scene<br>☐ Specific data (evidence) from the density gradient lab work is used to support the lake choice<br>☐ Evidence to support or not support the hypothesis for the cooler evidence uses specific examples from the data<br>☐ Where is the evidence leading so far?? Any suspects more likely than others at this point based on the evidence and suspect file information? Make sure you say why!! | Makes general, logical connections between ideas or events; mostly concrete in nature (3 of 4) | Makes superficial connections between ideas; thinking might be confused or incomplete (2 of 4) | Makes incorrect or no connections between ideas (1 of 4) | No work shown for this section |

## IV. Conclusion—Part II: The Delivery Truck Evidence

| Application | # | wgt | Exemplary (10) | At Standard (8) | In Progress (7) | Still Emerging (6) | No Evaluation (0) |
|---|---|---|---|---|---|---|---|
| Connecting Ideas | 1d | ½ | Makes insightful connections between ideas or events that might not be obvious—abstract thinking evident (4 of 4)<br>☐ The purpose is answered for if the police will be able to safely extract the sunken delivery truck from the lake without the volume of the airbag going over the maximum capacity<br>☐ Specific data (evidence) is used to support the whether or not the airbag will stay intact when the truck is retrieved from the lake<br>☐ Evidence to support or not support the hypothesis for the delivery truck evidence uses specific examples from the data<br>☐ Where is the evidence leading so far?? Any suspects more likely than others at this point based on the evidence and suspect file information? Make sure you say why!! | Makes general, logical connections between ideas or events; mostly concrete in nature (3 of 4) | Makes superficial connections between ideas; thinking might be confused or incomplete (2 of 4) | Makes incorrect or no connections between ideas (1 of 4) | No work shown for this section |

## V. Discussion Questions—Part I: The Cooler Evidence

| Application | # | wgt | Exemplary (10) | At Standard (8) | In Progress (7) | Still Emerging (6) | No Evaluation (0) |
|---|---|---|---|---|---|---|---|
| Supporting Ideas | 3b | ½ | Support used is varied, the best available, and strongly enhances audience understanding (4 of 4)<br>☐ Questions #1 is answered correctly and answer is supported with data to explain why<br>☐ Questions #2 is answered correctly and answer is supported with data to explain why<br>☐ Questions #3 is answered correctly and answer is supported with data to explain why<br>☐ Answers are written in complete sentences for all questions that require explanations | Support is accurate and sufficiently detailed—all basics evident (3 of 4) | Support is insufficient, inaccurate, or vague in places—enough to confuse audience somewhat (2 of 4) | Support is missing, inaccurate, or vague overall (1 of 4) | No work shown for this section |

## V. Discussion Questions—Part II: The Delivery Truck Evidence

| Application | # | wgt | Exemplary (10) | At Standard (8) | In Progress (7) | Still Emerging (6) | No Evaluation (0) |
|---|---|---|---|---|---|---|---|
| Supporting Ideas | 3b | ½ | Support used is varied, the best available, and strongly enhances audience understanding (4 of 4)<br>☐ Questions #1 is answered correctly and answer is supported with volume data to explain why<br>☐ Questions #2 is answered correctly connecting the graph to the correct gas law and answer is supported with data to explain why the graph shows the relationship stated<br>☐ Questions #3 is answered correctly connecting the graph to the correct gas law and answer is supported with data to explain why the graph shows the relationship stated<br>☐ Questions #4 is answered correctly and answer is supported with logical connections to the kinetic molecular theory to explain why | Support is accurate and sufficiently detailed—all basics evident (3 of 4) | Support is insufficient, inaccurate, or vague in places—enough to confuse audience somewhat (2 of 4) | Support is missing, inaccurate, or vague overall (1 of 4) | No work shown for this section |

## Overall Evidence Report Formatting

| Application | # | wgt | Exemplary (10) | At Standard (8) | In Progress (7) | Still Emerging (6) | No Evaluation (0) |
|---|---|---|---|---|---|---|---|
| Technology Applications | 1c | ½ | Technology used is best available and appropriate for the required research, data representation, interpretation, and communication of results. (4 of 4)<br>☐ Entire Lab Report is computer generated<br>☐ Lab Report is in an Outline Format<br>☐ The use of personal pronouns is non-evident<br>☐ Lab Report includes all sections required in the Lab Report Style Guide as required by the rubric | Technology was used for the required research, data representation, interpretation, and communication of results. (3 of 4) | Technology used was insufficient for the required research, data representation, interpretation, and communication of results. (2 of 4) | Evidence of Technology use is missing and/or insufficient (1 of 4) | No work shown for this section |

## Content Recall

| Application | # | wgt | Exemplary (10) | At Standard (8) | In Progress (7) | Still Emerging (6) | No Evaluation (0) |
|---|---|---|---|---|---|---|---|
| Content Recall | 1f | ½ | Recalls virtually all essential terms and factual information<br>☐ 0 Content Questions were asked to the instructor for the duration of this performance assessment | Recalls most essential terms and factual information<br>☐ 1 Content Question was asked to the instructor for the duration of this performance assessment | Recalls a minimum of essential terms and factual information<br>☐ 2 Content Questions were asked to the instructor for the duration of this performance assessment | Recalls virtually no essential terms and factual information<br>☐ 3 or more Content Questions were asked to the instructor for the duration of this performance assessment | No work shown for this section |

**Some things I think I did well on this assessment are:**

**Some things I still have questions about performance assessments, lab reports, this class, etc. are:**

**If I graded myself on this, my score would be a _____ /120, then divide that by 2 to get score out of 60 because each section is weighted by ½.**

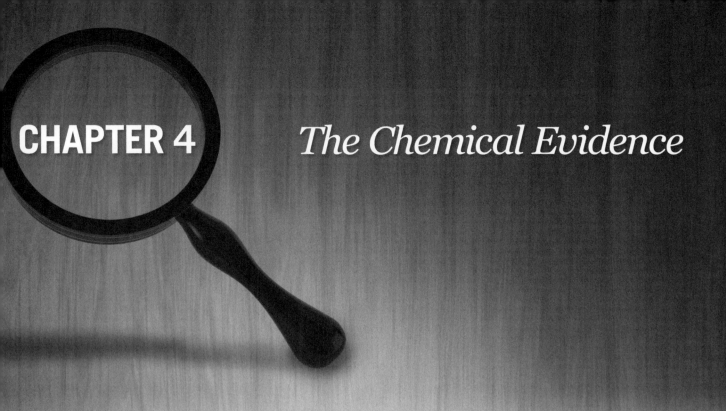

## CHEMISTRY CONTENT

- Empirical Formula
- Percent Composition
- Stoichiometry
- Mole to Gram Calculations
- Limiting Reactant
- Percent Yield

## NATIONAL SCIENCE EDUCATION STANDARDS ADDRESSED

Content Standard A: Science as Inquiry
Content Standard B: Physical Science
Content Standard G: History and Nature of Science

## CASE INFORMATION

Police have learned some additional information about the suspects involved in this case, and their relation to the victim. These details are provided in the Suspect File and have been summarized as follows: We now know that the victim, Kirsten K., worked for Elizabeth G., suspect #3, at her wedding cake business on the days when Kirsten was not working at the local hospital. Suspect #1, Harold M.,

recently had surgery on his back from an accident he had while working. Kirsten K., the victim, was his nurse during his stay at the hospital. Suspect #2, Gladys V., recently rented her lake house to Kirsten and her husband, Larry J., suspect #4, who was convicted for dealing drugs four years ago. Finally, Kirsten, the victim, was last seen delivering a wedding cake for a reception at a local hotel.

Based on the recycled cooler evidence and the abandoned truck analysis provided by your students, along with the new suspect information, police have decided to continue their investigation around the body of water that your students determined to be the crime scene. After an initial search of the crime scene, police have collected a number of samples of chemical evidence. They are asking your students to analyze that evidence to determine the type of chemical substances present and possibly match the substances at the crime scene to the suspects involved in the case. This performance assessment consists of four parts. In the first part, your students will analyze the chemical samples collected at the crime scene to determine the composition of each sample. In the second part, your students will match the chemical substances with the suspects in the case. In the third part, your students will determine the amount of moles of each substance.

Finally, in the fourth part, your students will perform some calculations to determine the unknown chemical sample and potentially link it to a suspect.

## Part I: The Delivery Truck and Crime Scene Evidence

In Part I of this assessment, students are given the percentages of each element found in the various substances from the crime scene and abandoned delivery truck analysis. By using the table Possible Compound Matches from their assessment, (Table 4.1, below) students can determine the chemical composition of each substance through two different methods. The first method by which students can determine the identity of the substance is to calculate the empirical formula of the compound by assuming that there is 100 g of the substance and then converting the percentages into grams. Students then convert each of the grams into moles for each element present in the substance and then divide each element amount by the smallest number of moles to find the ratio of elements. Finally, students multiply by a number to get the ratios to the lowest whole number ratio, or the empirical formula.

The second method students could use to solve for the type of substance found at the crime scene is to use the information provided in Table 2: Possible Compound Matches and calculate the percent composition of each of the substances to see which ones match the percentages given from the crime scene data.

No matter which way students choose to calculate the chemical matches, they will find that there are two unknown chemicals, one that is later identified at the end of this assessment and one that remains unknown until the last assessment of the forensics case (see Chapter 7: The Drug Lab Evidence). It will be determined to be caffeine, a substance that was being used to make a specific drug by

## TABLE 4.1

**POSSIBLE COMPOUND MATCHES***

| COMPOUNDS | CHEMICAL FORMULA | EVERYDAY USES |
|---|---|---|
| Acetaminophen | $C_8H_9NO_2$ | Painkiller (Tylenol) |
| Almond | $C_7H_6O$ | Flavoring |
| Aspartame | $C_{14}H_{18}N_2O_5$ | Artificial sweetener |
| Aspirin | $C_9H_8O_4$ | Painkiller |
| Cocaine | $C_{17}H_{21}NO_4$ | Narcotic, illegal |
| Codeine | $C_{18}H_{21}NO_3$ | Painkiller, prescription controlled |
| Curare | $C_{40}H_{44}N_4O$ | Poison |
| Ibuprofen | $C_{13}H_{18}O_2$ | Painkiller |
| Nitroglycerine | $C_3H_5N_3O_9$ | Explosive, heart medication |
| Trinitrotoluene | $C_7H_3N_3O_6$ | Explosive (TNT-dynamite) |
| Vanilla | $C_8H_8O_3$ | Flavoring |

* Data table adapted with permission from the *Journal of Chemical Education*, April 2003, 80(4): 407–408.

one of the suspects, Gerald V., who is not introduced until performance assessment #4 (see Chapter 6: The Weapon Analysis Evidence).

## Part II: The Suspect Evidence

In Part II of the assessment, students are trying to match substances found at the crime scene to substances that have been found on each of the suspects. By finding matches in this case, it puts the suspects at the crime scene and gives students direct evidence of who the police believe are the lead suspects at this point in the investigation. Based on the student findings and the new information presented in Suspect File B, the following reasoning may be used in relation to linking the chemicals to the suspects.

Students find that vanilla was in the abandoned delivery truck, which makes sense given that the victim was last seen delivering a cake to a local hotel and therefore may have transferred this chemical substance to the vehicle she was driving at the time. Also, the victim was at the crime scene, which is how the vanilla got transferred to that location. Harold M. was found to be carrying aspirin, which was also found at the crime scene; however, aspirin is a common chemical that can be purchased over the counter, so this does not necessarily put him directly at the crime scene. Harold M. also had surgery recently, according to the suspect file, so the aspirin could have been prescribed following his surgery, which would explain why he had the aspirin substance on him. Gladys V. was found to have the cocaine substance on her, which was also found at the crime scene. This is a more suspicious piece of evidence because of the illegal nature of the drug. Gladys V. is a retired pharmacist, which means she has an extensive knowledge about all types of drugs. Additionally, Larry J., husband of the victim, has been convicted for drug charges in the past. This may connect the two suspects since Larry J. and Kirsten K. were staying in Gladys V.'s lake house the week the victim went missing.

Sometimes students who choose to do the calculations using percent composition only solve for the percent composition of carbon instead of solving for the percentages of all the elements in the substances. Students are able to figure out the substances this way because the percent composition of the carbon is different for each possible chemical.

Suspect #3, Elizabeth G., is found to have acetaminophen and also a second unknown substance directly on her. While the unknown substance may seem suspicious in the beginning, students determine by the end of the assessment that the substance found on Elizabeth G. is just an ingredient that she uses in her cake shop. Larry J., suspect #4, is found to have nitroglycerine on him, but this substance can be used as a heart medicine as well, which fits with what we know about the suspect. Nitroglycerine was not found at the crime scene; however, the first unknown substance that was found at the crime scene was also found on Larry J., which may put him at the crime scene. Students will have to wait until the final assessment to determine what this substance is and how it fits with the overall conclusion of the case.

## Part III: The Amount of Chemical Substance

Part III of the assessment requires students to convert the grams of each substance found at the crime scene into moles of that substance. This part of the assessment does not add any evidence to the forensics case but shows the ability of the students to convert substances using metric conversions and mole conversions.

### Part IV: The Cake Shop Ingredients Analysis

Part IV of the assessment is a simulation calculation that provides the chemical reaction for the production of vanilla in Elizabeth G.'s cake shop. Students are able to use limiting reactant and percent yield within the reaction simulation calculations. While this part of the assessment does not lead to any evidence about the case directly, it does help students determine the second unknown substance found in Part II of this assessment, as it matches the excess reagent from the production of vanilla reaction. Suspect #3, Elizabeth G., is found to have this chemical on her, which makes sense since she owns a cake making business.

In the remaining pages of this chapter, you will find a teacher guide, student handout, suspect file, teacher guide, student lab report example, and grading rubric for Performance Assessment 2: The Chemical Evidence. More information about how to use the grading rubric for this and future performance assessments can be found in Appendix B.

# Teacher Guide:
# *The Chemical Evidence*

**Time:** 4–5 days
**Grades:** 11 and 12 (second-year chemistry)

## OBJECTIVES

1. Students will solve a forensics case using their knowledge of chemistry (for performance assessment #2 this includes balancing equations, mole calculations, stoichiometry, limiting reactants, percent yield, and molecular formulas).
2. Students will assemble their evidence and present their case at the end of the year.
3. Students will answer three questions:
   a. Identify the unknown chemicals based on their composition.
   b. Analyze the suspect residues to determine the chemicals found on them.
   c. Identify the limiting reactant, excess reactant, unknowns, and percent yield.

## PREPARATION

- Make copies of the student handouts packet including the suspect file B.
- No lab preparation is required for this assessment.

## THE LAB

Students use the scenario provided to calculate information that will provide evidence for their forensics case. The work that they do will be assembled as part of their evidence file, which will be maintained throughout the year.

## QUESTION GUIDELINES

For calculations, formulas, and work, see the student example at the end of the chapter.

### Part I

1. For calculations of each of the following, see the student example.
   a. Chemical A: vanilla
   b. Chemical B: vanilla
   c. Chemical C: cocaine
   d. Chemical D: aspirin
   e. Chemical E: unknown #1 (determined to be caffeine in Chapter 7)
2. The empirical formula of unknown #1 is $C_4H_5N_2O$.

### Part II

1. For calculations of each of the following, see the student example.
   a. Victim: vanilla
   b. Suspect #1—Harold M.: aspirin
   c. Suspect #2—Gladys V.: cocaine
   d. Suspect #3—Elizabeth G.: acetaminophen, unknown #2
   e. Suspect #4—Larry J.: nitroglycerine, unknown #1
2. The empirical formula for unknown #2 is $C_2H_2O_3$.

### *Part III*

1.  See student example for calculations

### *Part IV*

1.  $2C_7H_8O_2 + C_2H_2O_3 \rightarrow 2C_8H_8O_3 + H_2O$
2.  Limiting reactant: guaiacol, $C_7H_8O_2$; excess reactant: glyoxylic acid, $C_2H_2O_3$
3.  Theoretical yield: 5.13%
4.  Percent yield: 3.19%
5.  % composition matches unknown #2: glyoxylic acid

## Materials

*   Suspect File B
*   Student guide
*   Calculator

## TEACHER HINTS

*   The unknown chemical is found to be caffeine in Chapter 7. Students cannot determine it in this performance assessment because they only have the empirical formula.
*   This performance assessment includes a tremendous amount of calculations. I would recommend that the calculations are graded from the performance assessment packet so students don't have to retype all the calculations.
*   To figure out the chemicals in Part II of the assessment, students will not have to redo all the calculations if they are observant and notice that most of the percentages are the same as the percentages from Part I.

Name:_____ Class:_____ Date:_____

# The Case of Kirsten K.:
## *The Chemical Evidence*

## PART I: THE DELIVERY TRUCK AND CRIME SCENE EVIDENCE

### *Case Background*

Based on the evidence from the cooler sample, police have started looking for the victim at the lake you had specified. Police have scanned the area indicated, and you have been called to do further tests on samples found from what police believe to be the crime scene (even though the victim's body has not been found yet) to present new information about the victim and suspects. After analyzing the crime scene samples, you have found what could be important chemical evidence that may link the suspects to the crime scene. There were five distinct residues that were found and the percentage of each element found in them is listed below in Table 1.

### *Purpose*

Your investigation should help police to determine if the chemical analysis matches any of the suspects to the crime scene and how they may or may not be linked.

## TABLE 1

**PERCENTAGE OF EACH ELEMENT FOUND FROM THE CHEMICAL EVIDENCE**

| ABANDONED DELIVERY TRUCK | CARBON (C) | HYDROGEN (H) | NITROGEN (N) | OXYGEN (O) |
|---|---|---|---|---|
| Chemical A | 63.15 % | 5.30% | — | 31.55% |
| **CRIME SCENE** | **C** | **H** | **N** | **O** |
| Chemical B | 63.15 % | 5.30% | — | 31.55% |
| Chemical C | 67.31% | 6.98% | 4.62% | 21.10% |
| Chemical D | 60.00% | 4.48% | — | 35.53% |
| Chemical E | 49.48% | 5.15% | 28.87% | 16.50% |

## Procedure

Use the information provided to complete the following steps:

1. From the percentages listed in Table 1, find the formula for each of the Chemicals A-E.
2. Using Table 2 below and the percent compositions given in Table 1, determine the chemicals found on the victim.
3. If no match can be found, mark the chemical as unknown.

## Analysis: Calculations

1. Show calculations for finding the chemical formula for each compound:

   Chemical A:_____

   Chemical B: _____

   Chemical C: _____

   Chemical D:_____

   Chemical E: _____

## Data

### TABLE 2

**POSSIBLE COMPOUNDS MATCHES***

| COMPOUNDS | CHEMICAL FORMULA | EVERYDAY USES |
| --- | --- | --- |
| Acetaminophen | $C_8H_9NO_2$ | Painkiller (Tylenol) |
| Almond | $C_7H_6O$ | Flavoring |
| Aspartame | $C_{14}H_{18}N_2O_5$ | Artificial sweetner |
| Aspirin | $C_9H_8O_4$ | Painkiller |
| Cocaine | $C_{17}H_{21}NO_4$ | Narcotic, Illegal |
| Codeine | $C_{18}H_{21}NO_3$ | Painkiller, prescription controlled |
| Curare | $C_{40}H_{44}N_4O$ | Poison |
| Ibuprofen | $C_{13}H_{18}O_2$ | Painkiller |
| Nitroglycerine | $C_3H_5N_3O_9$ | Explosive, heart medication |
| Trinitrotoluene | $C_7H_3N_3O_6$ | Explosive (TNT-dynamite) |
| Vanilla | $C_8H_8O_3$ | Flavoring |

* Data table adapted with permission from the *Journal of Chemical Education*, April 2003, 80(4): 407–**408**.

2. Calculate the empirical formula for any unknown substances:

## Conclusion

List each of the chemicals and explain why you might expect to find each of these chemicals at the crime scene. This information should be based on the location of the crime scene given to police based on the evidence collected in the previous assessment.

_____
_____
_____
_____
_____

# PART II: THE SUSPECT EVIDENCE

## Background Information

Subsequent chemical analysis of clothing, blood, and skin samples from the four suspects and a piece of clothing believed to have belonged to the victim revealed the following information provided in Table 3.

## Analysis: Calculations

1. Show calculations for each of the chemicals found for each of the suspects below:

Victim: _____

Suspect #1:_____

Suspect #2:_____

Suspect #3:_____

Suspect #4:_____

## Data

### TABLE 3

**PERCENTAGE OF EACH ELEMENT FOUND IN THE CHEMICAL EVIDENCE FROM EACH SUSPECT**

|  | C | H | N | O |
|---|---|---|---|---|
| Victim | 63.15 % | 5.30% | — | 31.55% |
| Suspect #1 | 60.00% | 4.48% | — | 35.53% |
| Suspect #2 | 67.31% | 6.98% | 4.62% | 21.10% |
| Suspect #3 | 32.43% | 2.70% | — | 64.87% |
|  | 63.56% | 6.00% | 9.27% | 21.17% |
| Suspect #4 | 15.87% | 2.22% | 18.15% | 63.41% |
|  | 49.48% | 5.15% | 28.87% | 16.50% |

2. Calculate the empirical formula for any unknown substances:

## Conclusion

Determine if there is a connection between the chemicals found on the suspects in Part II and the information gained from the chemical analysis in Part I.

## PART III: THE AMOUNT OF CHEMICAL SUBSTANCE

### Background Information

Before the chemicals can be analyzed any further, the amount of each chemical found at the crime scene and from the suspects needs to be converted to the number of moles of each substance. You should be able to calculate the moles of each substance based on the following information in Table 4.

## TABLE 4

**AMOUNT OF CHEMICAL SUBSTANCE FROM CRIME SCENES AND SUSPECTS**

| ABANDONED DELIVERY TRUCK | AMOUNT FOUND | MOLES |
|---|---|---|
| Chemical A | 0.250 mg | |
| **CRIME SCENE** | **AMOUNT FOUND** | |
| Chemical B | 0.004 kg | |
| Chemical C | 1.35 mg | |
| Chemical D | 0.02 g | |
| Chemical E | 0.8 g | |
| **VICTIM AND SUSPECTS** | **AMOUNT FOUND** | |
| Victim | 0.03 g | |
| Suspect #1 | 0.09 g | |
| Suspect #2 | 2.5 mg | |
| Suspect #3 | 0.06 g | |
| | 1.2 mg | |
| Suspect #4 | 0.05 g | |
| | 0.001 kg | |

## Data

After calculating the number of moles of each substance, fill in the Table 4 with the correct amount.

## Conclusion

Which amounts were you unable to calculate and why? What does having an unknown mean for the investigation?

_____
_____
_____
_____
_____
_____
_____
_____
_____

# PART IV: THE CAKE SHOP INGREDIENTS ANALYSIS

## Background Information

After analyzing the chemicals further, it has been determined that some of the chemicals found at the crime scene (where the victim was believed to have been at one point) and on suspect #3 could have derived from the cake shop where both were employed. Further investigation shows that the day before the murder, the victim and suspect #3 were fully booked with requests for wedding cakes.

## Data

The cake shop, in order to keep their recipes secret, synthesizes their own vanilla flavoring for their cakes based on the following reaction:

$$C_7H_8O_2 + C_2H_2O_3 \rightarrow C_8H_8O_3 + H_2O$$
(guaiacol) (glyoxylic acid) (vanilla)

To verify the reaction done in the cake shop, the CSI chemical lab has simulated the experiment. They used 4.2 g of guaiacol and 6.8 g of glyoxylic acid.

## Analysis: Calculations

Using the information given, do the following calculations:

1. Show the balanced equation below.
2. Determine the limiting reactant.
3. Determine the theoretical yield of vanilla.
4. A 4.85 g sample of vanilla was produced from the reaction in the CSI chemical lab. Based on this information, calculate the % yield by comparing the experimental amount to the theoretical amount.
5. Does the chemical % composition of the excess reagent match any of the unknowns from Part I or Part II? If so, identify the unknown(s).

## Conclusion

Determine the connection, if any, between the unknowns and the crime scene. What else can you conclude about the case from the evidence presented through the calculations and from the new suspect information?

# SUSPECT FILE B

### Victim: Kirsten K.

- Helped Elizabeth G. with ther wedding cake business on the days when she wasn't working at the hospital
- Was last seen delivering a wedding cake for a reception at a local hoteL

### Suspect #1: Harold M.

- Just recently had surgery on his back from a work-related accident
- Kirsten K. was his nurse during his stay at the hospital for recovery

### Suspect #2: Gladys V.

- Rented the lake house out to the victim and her husband the week she went missing

### Suspect #3: Elizabeth G.

- Kirsten K. was an employee of hers

### Suspect #4: Larry J.

- Convicted for dealing drugs four years ago

Name:_____ Class:_____ Date:_____

# Student Lab Report Example:
## *The Chemical Evidence*

## I. INTRODUCTION

### (A) Background Information

The victim, Kirsten K., was confirmed to have helped Elizabeth G. with her wedding cake business when she was not working in the hospital. She was last seen delivering a cake for Elizabeth G. at a local hotel. Elizabeth G.'s business makes its own special formula for their vanilla flavoring. New information about the suspects has surfaced; such as Kirsten K. was Harold M.'s nurse while he was at the local hospital for back surgery. Gladys V. was the owner of the lake house that Kristen and her husband rented the week that she went missing. And Larry J. was convicted for dealing drugs four years ago. One chemical was discovered in the sunken delivery truck after it was extracted from the lake. And, four other chemicals were discovered around Clinton Lake where police now believe the victim was abducted. Tests will be done on each chemical to find out what it is and how much there was of each; then it can help connect the suspects to actually being at the crime scene.

### (B) Purpose

To link substances found at the crime scene to the possible suspects to place specific suspects at the scene of the crime.

## II. DATA

### Part I: The Delivery Truck and Crime Scene Evidence

**PERCENTAGE CHEMICALS FOUND IN DELIVERY TRUCK AND AT CRIME SCENE**

| | C | H | N | O |
|---|---|---|---|---|
| **Sunken Delivery Truck** | | | | |
| **Chemical A** Vanilla ($C_8H_8O_3$) | 63.15% | 5.30% | — | 31.55% |
| **Crime Scene** | | | | |
| **Chemical B** Vanilla ($C_8H_8O_3$) | 63.15% | 5.30% | — | 31.55% |
| **Chemical C** Cocaine ($C_{17}H_{21}NO_4$) | 67.31% | 6.98% | 4.62% | 21.10% |
| **Chemical D** Aspirin ($C_9H_8O_4$) | 60.00% | 4.48% | — | 35.53% |
| **Chemical E** Unknown #1 | 49.48% | 5.15% | 28.87% | 16.50% |

### Part II: The Suspect Evidence

**PERCENTAGE OF CHEMICALS FOUND ON EACH OF THE SUSPECTS**

| | C | H | N | O |
|---|---|---|---|---|
| **Victim** Vanilla ($C_8H_8O_3$) | 63.15% | 5.30% | — | 31.55% |
| **Suspect #1** Aspirin ($C_9H_8O_4$) | 60.00% | 4.48% | — | 35.53% |
| **Suspect #2** Cocaine ($C_{17}H_{21}NO_4$) | 67.31% | 6.98% | 4.62% | 21.10% |
| **Suspect #3** Unknown #2 | 32.43% | 2.70% | — | 64.87% |
| Acetaminophen ($C_8H_9NO_2$) | 63.56% | 6.00% | 9.27% | 21.17% |
| **Suspect #4** Nitroglycerine ($C_3H_5N_3O_9$) | 15.87% | 2.22% | 18.15% | 63.41% |
| Unknown #1 | 49.48% | 5.15% | 28.87% | 16.5% |

## Part III: The Amount of Chemical Substance

**AMOUNT OF CHEMICAL FOUND IN DELIVERY TRUCK, AT CRIME SCENE AND ON SUSPECTS**

| SUNKEN DELIVERY TRUCK | AMOUNT FOUND | MOLES |
|---|---|---|
| Chemical A | 0.250 mg | $1.6 \times 10^{-6}$ |
| **CRIME SCENE** | **AMOUNT FOUND** | **MOLES** |
| Chemical B | 0.004 kg | 0.026 |
| Chemical C | 1.35 mg | $4.45 \times 10^{-6}$ |
| Chemical D | 0.02 g | $1.1 \times 10^{-4}$ |
| Chemical E | 0.8 g | Unknown #1 |
| **VICTIM AND SUSPECTS** | **AMOUNT FOUND** | **MOLES** |
| Victim | 0.03 g | $1.97 \times 10^{-4}$ |
| Suspect #1 | 0.09 g | $5 \times 10^{-4}$ |
| Suspect #2 | 2.5 mg | $8.25 \times 10^{-6}$ |
| Suspect #3 | 0.06 g<br>1.2 mg | Unknown #2;<br>$7.9 \times 10^{-6}$ |
| Suspect #4 | 0.05g<br>0.001kg | $2.20 \times 10^{-4}$<br>Unknown #1 |

## III. ANALYSIS: CALCULATIONS

### Part I: The Delivery Truck and Crime Scene Evidence

**Chemical A:** Vanilla ($C_8H_8O_3$)

| ELEMENT SYMBOL | GRAMS TO MOLES CALCULATION | DIVIDE BY SMALLER # OF MOLES | CALCULATE WHOLE # RATIO | RATIO |
|---|---|---|---|---|
| C | 63.15 g C x $\frac{1\ mole\ C}{12.01\ g\ C}$ = 5.26 moles C | $\frac{5.26\ moles}{1.97\ moles}$ = 2.66 | 2.66 x 3 = 8 | 8 |
| H | 5.30 g H x $\frac{1\ mole\ C}{1.01\ g\ C}$ = 5.25 moles H | $\frac{5.25\ moles}{1.97\ moles}$ = 2.66 | 2.66 x 3 = 8 | 8 |
| O | 31.55 g O x $\frac{1\ mole\ C}{16.00\ g\ C}$ = 1.97 moles O | $\frac{1.97\ moles}{1.97\ moles}$ = 1 | 1 x 3 = 8 | 3 |

**Chemical B:** Vanilla ($C_8H_8O_3$)

| ELEMENT SYMBOL | GRAMS TO MOLES CALCULATION | DIVIDE BY SMALLER # OF MOLES | CALCULATE WHOLE # RATIO | RATIO |
|---|---|---|---|---|
| C | 63.15 g C x $\frac{1\ mole\ C}{12.01\ g\ C}$ = 5.26 moles C | $\frac{5.26\ moles}{1.97\ moles}$ = 2.66 | 2.66 x 3 = 8 | 8 |
| H | 5.30 g H x $\frac{1\ mole\ C}{1.01\ g\ C}$ = 5.25 moles H | $\frac{5.25\ moles}{1.97\ moles}$ = 2.66 | 2.66 x 3 = 8 | 8 |
| O | 31.55 g O x $\frac{1\ mole\ C}{16.00\ g\ C}$ = 1.97 moles O | $\frac{1.97\ moles}{1.97\ moles}$ = 1 | 1 x 3 = 8 | 3 |

**Chemical C:** Cocaine ($C_{17}H_{21}NO_4$)

| ELEMENT SYMBOL | GRAMS TO MOLES CALCULATION | DIVIDE BY SMALLER # OF MOLES | CALCULATE WHOLE # RATIO | RATIO |
|---|---|---|---|---|
| C | 67.31 g C x $\frac{1\ mole\ C}{12.01\ g\ C}$ = 5.26 moles C | $\frac{5.60\ moles}{0.33\ moles}$ = 17 | — | 17 |
| H | 6.98 g H x $\frac{1\ mole\ C}{1.01\ g\ C}$ = 5.25 moles H | $\frac{6.91\ moles}{0.33\ moles}$ = 21 | — | 21 |
| N | 4.62 g N x $\frac{1\ mole\ C}{14.01\ g\ C}$ = 1.97 moles N | $\frac{0.33\ moles}{0.33\ moles}$ = 1 | — | 1 |
| O | 31.55 g O x $\frac{1\ mole\ C}{16.00\ g\ C}$ = 1.97 moles O | $\frac{1.32\ moles}{0.33\ moles}$ = 4 | — | 4 |

**Chemical D:** Aspirin ($C_9H_8O_4$)

| ELEMENT SYMBOL | GRAMS TO MOLES CALCULATION | DIVIDE BY SMALLER # OF MOLES | CALCULATE WHOLE # RATIO | RATIO |
|---|---|---|---|---|
| C | $60.00 \text{ g C} \times \dfrac{1 \text{ mole C}}{12.01 \text{ g C}} = 5.00 \text{ moles C}$ | $\dfrac{5.00 \text{ moles}}{2.22 \text{ moles}} = 2.25$ | $2.25 \times 4 = 9$ | 9 |
| H | $4.48 \text{ g H} \times \dfrac{1 \text{ mole C}}{1.01 \text{ g C}} = 4.44 \text{ moles H}$ | $\dfrac{4.44 \text{ moles}}{2.22 \text{ moles}} = 2$ | $2 \times 4 = 8$ | 8 |
| O | $35.53 \text{ g O} \times \dfrac{1 \text{ mole C}}{16.00 \text{ g C}} = 2.22 \text{ moles O}$ | $\dfrac{2.22 \text{ moles}}{2.22 \text{ moles}} = 1$ | $1 \times 4 = 4$ | 4 |

**Chemical E:** Unknown #1 (Empirical Formula: $C_4H_5N_2O$)

| ELEMENT SYMBOL | GRAMS TO MOLES CALCULATION | DIVIDE BY SMALLER # OF MOLES | CALCULATE WHOLE # RATIO | RATIO |
|---|---|---|---|---|
| C | $49.48 \text{ g C} \times \dfrac{1 \text{ mole C}}{12.01 \text{ g C}} = 5.26 \text{ moles C}$ | $\dfrac{4.12 \text{ moles}}{1 \text{ mole}} = 4.12$ | — | 4 |
| H | $5.15 \text{ g H} \times \dfrac{1 \text{ mole C}}{1.01 \text{ g C}} = 5.25 \text{ moles H}$ | $\dfrac{5.10 \text{ moles}}{1 \text{ mole}} = 5.10$ | — | 5 |
| N | $28.87 \text{ g N} \times \dfrac{1 \text{ mole C}}{14.01 \text{ g C}} = 1.97 \text{ moles N}$ | $\dfrac{2.06 \text{ moles}}{1 \text{ mole}} = 2.06$ | — | 2 |
| O | $16.5 \text{ g O} \times \dfrac{1 \text{ mole C}}{16.00 \text{ g C}} = 1.97 \text{ moles O}$ | $\dfrac{1.0 \text{ moles}}{1 \text{ mole}} = 1$ | — | 1 |

### Part II: The Suspect Evidence

**Victim:** Kirsten K. = Vanilla ($C_8H_8O_3$)

| ELEMENT SYMBOL | GRAMS TO MOLES CALCULATION | DIVIDE BY SMALLER # OF MOLES | CALCULATE WHOLE # RATIO | RATIO |
|---|---|---|---|---|
| C | $63.15 \text{ g C} \times \dfrac{1 \text{ mole C}}{12.01 \text{ g C}} = 5.26$ moles C | $\dfrac{5.26 \text{ moles}}{1.97 \text{ moles}} = 2.66$ | $2.66 \times 3 = 8$ | 8 |
| H | $5.30 \text{ g H} \times \dfrac{1 \text{ mole C}}{1.01 \text{ g C}} = 5.25$ moles H | $\dfrac{5.25 \text{ moles}}{1.97 \text{ moles}} = 2.66$ | $2.66 \times 3 = 8$ | 8 |
| O | $31.55 \text{ g O} \times \dfrac{1 \text{ mole C}}{16.00 \text{ g C}} = 1.97$ moles O | $\dfrac{1.97 \text{ moles}}{1.97 \text{ moles}} = 1$ | $1 \times 3 = 3$ | 3 |

**Suspect #1:** Harold M. = Aspirin ($C_9H_8O_4$)

| ELEMENT SYMBOL | GRAMS TO MOLES CALCULATION | DIVIDE BY SMALLER # OF MOLES | CALCULATE WHOLE # RATIO | RATIO |
|---|---|---|---|---|
| C | $60.00 \text{ g C} \times \dfrac{1 \text{ mole C}}{12.01 \text{ g C}} = 5.00$ moles C | $\dfrac{5.00 \text{ moles}}{2.22 \text{ moles}} = 2.25$ | $2.25 \times 4 = 9$ | 9 |
| H | $4.48 \text{ g H} \times \dfrac{1 \text{ mole C}}{1.01 \text{ g C}} = 4.44$ moles H | $\dfrac{4.44 \text{ moles}}{2.22 \text{ moles}} = 2$ | $2 \times 4 = 8$ | 8 |
| O | $35.53 \text{ g O} \times \dfrac{1 \text{ mole C}}{16.00 \text{ g C}} = 2.22$ moles O | $\dfrac{2.22 \text{ moles}}{2.22 \text{ moles}} = 1$ | $1 \times 4 = 4$ | 4 |

**Suspect #2:** Gladys V. = Cocaine ($C_{17}H_{21}NO_4$)

| ELEMENT SYMBOL | GRAMS TO MOLES CALCULATION | DIVIDE BY SMALLER # OF MOLES | CALCULATE WHOLE # RATIO | RATIO |
|---|---|---|---|---|
| C | $67.31 \text{ g C} \times \dfrac{1 \text{ mole C}}{12.01 \text{ g C}} = 5.26$ moles C | $\dfrac{5.60 \text{ moles}}{0.33 \text{ moles}} = 17$ | — | 17 |
| H | $6.98 \text{ g H} \times \dfrac{1 \text{ mole C}}{1.01 \text{ g C}} = 5.25$ moles H | $\dfrac{6.91 \text{ moles}}{0.33 \text{ moles}} = 21$ | — | 21 |
| N | $4.62 \text{ g N} \times \dfrac{1 \text{ mole C}}{14.01 \text{ g C}} = 1.97$ moles N | $\dfrac{0.33 \text{ moles}}{0.33 \text{ moles}} = 1$ | — | 1 |
| O | $31.55 \text{ g O} \times \dfrac{1 \text{ mole C}}{16.00 \text{ g C}} = 1.97$ moles O | $\dfrac{1.32 \text{ moles}}{0.33 \text{ moles}} = 4$ | — | 4 |

**Suspect #3:** Elizabeth G. = Unknown #2 ($C_2H_2O_3$)

| ELEMENT SYMBOL | GRAMS TO MOLES CALCULATION | DIVIDE BY SMALLER # OF MOLES | CALCULATE WHOLE # RATIO | RATIO |
|---|---|---|---|---|
| C | $32.43 \text{ g C} \times \dfrac{1 \text{ mole C}}{12.01 \text{ g C}} = 2.70 \text{ moles C}$ | $\dfrac{2.70 \text{ moles}}{2.67 \text{ moles}} = 1$ | $1 \times 2 = 2$ | 2 |
| H | $2.70 \text{ g H} \times \dfrac{1 \text{ mole C}}{1.01 \text{ g C}} = \text{moles H}$ | $\dfrac{2.67 \text{ moles}}{2.67 \text{ moles}} = 1$ | $1 \times 2 = 3$ | 2 |
| O | $64.87 \text{ g O} \times \dfrac{1 \text{ mole C}}{16.00 \text{ g C}} = \text{moles O}$ | $\dfrac{4.00 \text{ moles}}{2.67 \text{ moles}} = 1.5$ | $1.5 \times 2 = 3$ | 3 |

**Suspect #3:** Elizabeth G. = Acetaminophen ($C_8H_9NO_2$)

| ELEMENT SYMBOL | GRAMS TO MOLES CALCULATION | DIVIDE BY SMALLER # OF MOLES | CALCULATE WHOLE # RATIO | RATIO |
|---|---|---|---|---|
| C | $63.56 \text{ g C} \times \dfrac{1 \text{ mole C}}{12.01 \text{ g C}} = 5.29 \text{ moles C}$ | $\dfrac{5.29 \text{ moles}}{0.66 \text{ moles}} = 8$ | — | 8 |
| H | $6.00 \text{ g H} \times \dfrac{1 \text{ mole C}}{1.01 \text{ g C}} = 5.94 \text{ moles H}$ | $\dfrac{5.94 \text{ moles}}{0.66 \text{ moles}} = 9$ | — | 9 |
| N | $9.27 \text{ g N} \times \dfrac{1 \text{ mole C}}{14.01 \text{ g C}} = 0.66 \text{ moles N}$ | $\dfrac{0.66 \text{ moles}}{0.66 \text{ moles}} = 1$ | — | 1 |
| O | $21.17 \text{ g O} \times \dfrac{1 \text{ mole C}}{16.00 \text{ g C}} = 1.32 \text{ moles O}$ | $\dfrac{1.32 \text{ moles}}{0.66 \text{ moles}} = 2$ | — | 2 |

**Suspect #4:** Larry J. = Nitroglycerine ($C_3H_5N_3O_9$)

| ELEMENT SYMBOL | GRAMS TO MOLES CALCULATION | DIVIDE BY SMALLER # OF MOLES | CALCULATE WHOLE # RATIO | RATIO |
|---|---|---|---|---|
| C | $15.87 \text{ g C} \times \dfrac{1 \text{ mole C}}{12.01 \text{ g C}} = 1.32 \text{ moles C}$ | $\dfrac{1.32 \text{ moles}}{1.30 \text{ moles}} = 1$ | $1 \times 3 = 3$ | 3 |
| H | $2.22 \text{ g H} \times \dfrac{1 \text{ mole C}}{1.01 \text{ g C}} = 2.20 \text{ moles H}$ | $\dfrac{2.20 \text{ moles}}{1.30 \text{ moles}} = 9$ | $1.7 \times 3 = 5$ | 5 |
| N | $18.15 \text{ g C} \times \dfrac{1 \text{ mole C}}{14.01 \text{ g C}} = 1.30 \text{ moles N}$ | $\dfrac{1.30 \text{ moles}}{1.30 \text{ moles}} = 1$ | $1 \times 3 = 3$ | 3 |
| O | $1.65 \text{ g O} \times \dfrac{1 \text{ mole C}}{16.00 \text{ g C}} = 3.96 \text{ moles O}$ | $\dfrac{3.96 \text{ moles}}{1.30 \text{ moles}} = 1$ | $3 \times 3 = 3$ | 9 |

**Suspect #4:** Larry J. = Unknown #1 ($C_4H_5N_2O$)

| ELEMENT SYMBOL | GRAMS TO MOLES CALCULATION | DIVIDE BY SMALLER # OF MOLES | CALCULATE WHOLE # RATIO | RATIO |
|---|---|---|---|---|
| C | $49.48 \text{ g C} \times \dfrac{1 \text{ mole C}}{12.01 \text{ g C}} = 5.26$ moles C | $\dfrac{4.12 \text{ moles}}{1 \text{ mole}} = 4.12$ | — | 4 |
| H | $5.15 \text{ g H} \times \dfrac{1 \text{ mole C}}{1.01 \text{ g C}} = 5.25$ moles H | $\dfrac{5.10 \text{ moles}}{1 \text{ mole}} = 5.10$ | — | 5 |
| N | $28.87 \text{ g N} \times \dfrac{1 \text{ mole C}}{14.01 \text{ g C}} = 1.97$ moles N | $\dfrac{2.06 \text{ moles}}{1 \text{ mole}} = 2.06$ | — | 2 |
| O | $16.5 \text{ g O} \times \dfrac{1 \text{ mole C}}{16.00 \text{ g C}} = 1.97$ moles O | $\dfrac{1.0 \text{ moles}}{1 \text{ mole}} = 1$ | — | 1 |

## Part III: The Amount of Chemical Substance

Chemical A

$$\left(\frac{.250 \text{ mg}}{}\right)\left(\frac{1000 \text{ g}}{1 \text{ kg}}\right)\left(\frac{1 \text{ mole}}{152 \text{ g}}\right) = 1.6 \times 10^{-6} \text{ moles}$$

Chemical B

$$\left(\frac{0.004 \text{ kg}}{}\right)\left(\frac{1000 \text{ g}}{1 \text{ kg}}\right)\left(\frac{1 \text{ mole}}{152 \text{ g}}\right) = 0.263 \text{ moles}$$

Chemical C

$$\left(\frac{1.35 \text{ g}}{}\right)\left(\frac{1 \text{ g}}{1000 \text{ mg}}\right)\left(\frac{1 \text{ mole}}{303 \text{ g}}\right) = 4.45 \times 10^{-6} \text{ moles}$$

Chemical D

$$\left(\frac{0.02 \text{ g}}{}\right)\left(\frac{1 \text{ mole}}{180 \text{ g}}\right) = 1.1 \times 10^{-4} \text{ moles}$$

Chemical E

Unknown 1, so cannot be calculated because only the empirical formula is known and may or may not be the molecular formula

Victim

$$\left(\frac{0.03 \text{ g}}{}\right)\left(\frac{1 \text{ mole}}{152 \text{ g}}\right) = 1.97 \times 10^{-4} \text{ moles}$$

Suspect #1

$$\left(\frac{.09 \text{ g}}{180 \text{ g}}\right)\left(1 \text{ mole}\right) = 5 \times 10^{-4} \text{ moles}$$

Suspect #2

$$\left(\frac{2.50 \text{ mg}}{}\right)\left(\frac{1 \text{ g}}{1000 \text{ mg}}\right)\left(\frac{1 \text{ mole}}{303 \text{ g}}\right) = 8.25 \times 10^{-6} \text{ moles}$$

Suspect #3 (unknown #2)

$$\left(\frac{0.06 \text{ g}}{}\right)\left(\frac{1 \text{ mole}}{74 \text{ g}}\right) = 8.1 \times 10^{-4} \text{ moles}$$

**Suspect #3**

$$\left(\frac{1.2\ mg}{}\right)\left(\frac{1\ g}{1000\ mg}\right)\left(\frac{1\ mole}{155g}\right) = 7.74 \times 10^{-6}$$

**Suspect #4**

$$\left(\frac{0.05\ g}{}\right)\left(\frac{1\ mole}{227\ g}\right) = 2.20 \times 10^{-4}$$

**Suspect #4**

0.001 kg Unknown #1, so cannot be calculated because only the empirical formula is known and may or may not be the molecular formula

## Part IV: The Cake Shop Ingredients Analysis
### Balanced equation

$$2C_7H_8O_2 + 1C_2H_2O_3 = 2C_8H_8O_3 + 1H_2O$$

### Limiting reactant

| Reactant | given | need |
|----------|-------|------|
| $C_7H_8O_2$ | 4.2 | 23 |
| $C_2H_2O_3$ | 6.8 | 1.3 |

$$\left(\frac{4.2\ g\ C_7H_8O_2}{}\right)\left(\frac{1\,mole\ C_7H_8O_2}{124\ g\ C_7H_8O_2}\right)\left(\frac{1\,mole\ C_2H_2O_3}{2\ mole\ C_7H_8O_2}\right)\left(\frac{74\ g\ C_2H_2O_3}{1\,mole\ C_2H_2O_3}\right) = 1.3\ g\ C_2H_2O_3$$

$$\left(\frac{6.8\ g\ C_2H_2O_3}{}\right)\left(\frac{1\,mole\ C_2H_2O_3}{74\ g\ C_2H_2O_3}\right)\left(\frac{2\,mole\ C_7H_8O_2}{2\,mole\ C_2H_2O_3}\right)\left(\frac{124\ g\ C_7H_8O_2}{1\,mole\ C_7H_8O_2}\right) = 23\ g\ C_7H_8O_2$$

Limiting Reactant: $C_7H_8O_2$

Excess Reagent: $C_2H_2O_3$

### Theoretical yield of vanilla

$$\left(\frac{4.2\ g\ C_7H_8O_2}{}\right)\left(\frac{1\,mole\ C_7H_8O_2}{124\ g\ C_7H_8O_2}\right)\left(\frac{2\,mole\ C_8H_8O_3}{2\ mole\ C_7H_8O_2}\right)\left(\frac{152\ g\ C_8H_8O_3}{1\,mole\ C_8H_8O_3}\right) = 5.1\ g\ C_8H_8O_3$$

### Percent yield of a 4.85 g sample of vanilla

$$\frac{Actual}{Theoretical} \times 100 \qquad \frac{4.85}{5.1} \times 100 = 95\%\ yield$$

### Matching Chemicals

The excess reagent, glyoxylic acid ($C_2H_2O_3$), matches the chemical percent composition and empirical formula for the unknown #2 found on Elizabeth G., suspect #2. This would make sense that this chemical was found on Elizabeth G. since vanilla is synthesized in her cake shop.

# IV. CONCLUSION

## Part I: The Delivery Truck and Crime Scene Evidence

List each of the chemicals and explain why you might expect to find each of these chemicals at the crime scene. This information should be based on the location of the crime scene given to police based on the evidence collected in the previous assessment.

√ Vanilla: This chemical could be found at the crime scene because Kirsten K. was last seen dropping off a cake at a reception with a cake containing the chemical vanilla. The fact that vanilla was also found in the delivery truck makes sense, since this ingredient is in many cakes that are delivered using the truck that was found sunken in Clinton Lake.

√ Cocaine: The cocaine that was found could have possibly been Larry J.'s, who was convicted for dealing drugs four years ago.

√ Aspirin: Harold M. could have been taking aspirin to relieve some of the pain. But aspirin is an over the counter drug and can be bought by anyone.

√ Unknown #1: We were unable to calculate the molecular formula of chemical E, which was found at the crime scene. It will be important to determine what Chemical E is to determine its importance in solving the case of Kirsten K.

## Part II: The Suspect Evidence

Determine if there is a connection between the chemicals found on the suspects in Part II and the information gained from the chemical analysis in Part I.

√ Victim's Clothing: Vanilla was also found on the piece of clothing at the crime scene that was believed to have belonged to the victim. This piece of clothing being left at the crime scene may indicate that there may have been a struggle as Kirsten K. was abducted.

√ Harold M.: Aspirin found on Harold M. Harold M. has just had back surgery. Aspirin is not a prescription drug so the fact the aspirin was at the crime scene and on Harold M. does not actually place him at the crime scene.

√ Gladys V.: Cocaine was found on Gladys V. and also at the crime scene. This is extremely suspicious just because of cocaine being an illegal drug. The fact that Gladys V. is a retired pharmacist means she would have an extensive knowledge of both legal and illegal drugs. Larry J. had a drug conviction in his past, so maybe Gladys V. and Larry J. are connected somehow with the buying and selling of drugs. Gladys V. should be questioned further about why she would have an illegal drug on her that was also found at the crime scene. Even if she was not involved in the abduction of the victim, Kirsten, police may discover other illegal activity surrounding Gladys V. and her lake house.

√ Elizabeth G.: Unknown #2 and Acetaminophen were both found on Elizabeth G. Neither chemical is suspicious at this point because unknown #2 is later discovered to be a reactant in the production of vanilla in Elizabeth's cake shop and acetaminophen is an over the counter drug anyone can purchase. Neither of the chemicals found on Elizabeth G. was found at the crime scene.

√ Larry Jensen: Nitroglycerine and Unknown #1 were both found on Larry J. Nitroglycerine is used mainly for a heart medicine or an explosive. Larry J. could have possibly been using nitroglycerine to destroy evidence, like the cooler, if he was trying to abduct his wife and wanted to blow up the evidence. Police would need to look into Larry J.'s medical history to see if he had heart problems in the past that he would need to be using a prescription drug, like nitroglycerine. The same Unknown #1 was found at the crime scene. Even though it is not known yet what Unknown #1 is, the fact that it was found at the crime scene would increase Larry J's likelihood of being a prime suspect in the abduction of Kirsten K., the victim.

## Part III: The Amount of Chemical Substance

Which amounts were you unable to calculate and why? What does having an unknown mean for the investigation?

At this time the amounts for the Unknown #1 and Unknown #2 cannot be calculated because only the empirical formulas are known. If the chemical formula is the same as the empirical formula then the molar mass can be added up and calculated. But without knowing if the formulas match, it is not possible to calculate the moles of each of the unknowns at this point in the investigation.

Having an unknown means that there are still some pieces of evidence that need to be connected for this investigation. It is important to be able to find out what the unknowns are to be able to determine exactly how they connect each suspect to this investigation.

## Part IV: The Cake Shop Ingredients Analysis

Determine the connection, if any, between the unknowns and the crime scene. What else can you conclude about the case from the evidence presented through the calculations and from the new suspect information?

1. Unknown #2 is determined to be glyoxylic acid, a chemical that Elizabeth G. uses as a reactant in her cake shop to produce vanilla for her wedding cakes. This is logical that Elizabeth G. would have this chemical found on her and since it wasn't at the crime scene, it does not need to be investigated further because there is no obvious link between the chemicals found on her and the crime scene.

2. The prime suspect at this point would be the victim's husband, Larry J. He had an unknown chemical on him that was also found at the crime scene. It is important for police to determine exactly what the unknown chemical is to see if it links Larry's past drug usage to the current crime that has been committed. Also, further questioning of Gladys V. needs to happen for police to determine why she would have an illegal drug on her that was also found at the crime scene.

# GRADING RUBRIC B

Name _____

Score _____ /50          _____ %          Grade _____

## I. Introduction

| Application | # | weight (wgt) | Exemplary (10) | At Standard (8) | In Progress (7) | Still Emerging (6) | No Evaluation (0) |
|---|---|---|---|---|---|---|---|
| Defining Problems | 1a | * | Makes insightful connections between ideas or events that might not be obvious; abstract thinking evident (4 of 4)<br><br>☐ **Background Information** includes important information about the suspects, including new information that may connect to the findings of the last study<br>☐ **Background Information** includes an explanation of what tests will be done in the chemical analysis tests<br>☐ **Background Information** includes an explanation of what each test in each part (I–IV) is going to hopefully prove as it relates to the case<br>NOTE** only one background section is needed for this entire assessment<br>☐ Purpose is clearly stated and correct | Makes general, logical connections between ideas or events; mostly concrete in nature (3 of 4) | Makes superficial connections between ideas; thinking might be confused or incomplete (2 of 4) | Makes incorrect or no connections between ideas (1 of 4) | No work shown for this section |

## II. Data

| Application | # | wgt | Exemplary (10) | At Standard (8) | In Progress (7) | Still Emerging (6) | No Evaluation (0) |
|---|---|---|---|---|---|---|---|
| Interpreting Models | 1b | * | Interprets visuals or models at a complex level (5 of 5)<br>☐ Data from **Table 1** and **Table 2** are reconstructed to show which compounds from Table 2 match each of the 5 chemical percentages listed in Table 1<br>☐ Data from **Table 1, Table 2,** and **Table 3** are reconstructed to show a connection between the chemicals found from the suspects to the chemicals found at the crime scene and the abandoned car<br>☐ Data **Table 4** is filled in to include the amount of moles<br>NOTE** 3 total data tables are needed for this entire assessment<br>☐ Completed data tables include a relevant **title** explaining the data sets and correct **labels/units** are used for all columns and rows in the data table where applicable | Interprets visuals or models at a general level (3 of 4) | Interpretation of visual or model contains errors that restrict understanding (2 of 4) | Shows fundamental errors in use and understanding of visual (1 of 4) | No work turned in for this section |

## III. Analysis: No Graph Needed
## III. Analysis: Part I: The Delivery Truck and Crime Scene Evidence—Chemical Calculations

| Application | # | wgt | Exemplary (10) | At Standard (8) | In Progress (7) | Still Emerging (6) | No Evaluation (0) |
|---|---|---|---|---|---|---|---|
| Problem Calculations | 2a | ½ | All essential information is evident through well-organized work while justifying the solution (5 of 5)<br>☐ Calculations for **Chemical A** are complete, correct, and all work was shown including units for all numbers throughout calculation<br>☐ Calculations for **Chemical B** are complete, correct, and all work was shown including units for all numbers throughout calculation | Most essential information is evident through organized work while leading to the solution (4 of 5) | Minimum information is evident through work with a solution present (3 of 4) | Work is extremely unorganized with no solution present (1–2 of 4) | No work shown for this section |

| | Exemplary (10) | At Standard (8) | In Progress (7) | Still Emerging (6) | No Evaluation (0) |
|---|---|---|---|---|---|
| (continued) | ☐ Calculations for **Chemical C** are complete, correct, and all work was shown including units for all numbers throughout calculation<br>☐ Calculations for **Chemical D** are complete, correct, and all work was shown including units for all numbers throughout calculation<br>☐ Calculations for **Chemical E** are complete, correct, and all work was shown including units for all numbers throughout calculation | | | Work is extremely unorganized with no solution present (1–2 of 4) | No work shown for this section |

## III. Analysis: Part II: The Suspect Evidence—Suspect Calculations

| Application | # | wgt | Exemplary (10) | At Standard (8) | In Progress (7) | Still Emerging (6) | No Evaluation (0) |
|---|---|---|---|---|---|---|---|
| Problem Calculations | 2a | ½ | All essential information is evident through well-organized work while justifying the solution (5 of 5)<br>☐ Calculations for **Victim** are complete, correct, and all work was shown including units for all numbers throughout calculation<br>☐ Calculations for **Suspect #1** are complete, correct, and all work was shown including units for all numbers throughout calculation<br>☐ Calculations for **Suspect #2** are complete, correct, and all work was shown including units for all numbers throughout calculation<br>☐ Calculations for **Suspect #3** are complete, correct, and all work was shown including units for all numbers throughout calculation<br>☐ Calculations for **Suspect #4** are complete, correct, and all work was shown including units for all numbers throughout calculation | Most essential information is evident through organized work while leading to the solution (4 of 5) | Minimum information is evident through work with a solution present (3 of 4) | Work is extremely unorganized with no solution present (1–2 of 4) | No work shown for this section |

## III. Analysis: Part III: The Amount of Chemical Substance—Mole Calculations

| Application | # | wgt | Exemplary (10) | At Standard (8) | In Progress (7) | Still Emerging (6) | No Evaluation (0) |
|---|---|---|---|---|---|---|---|
| Problem Calculations | 2a | ½ | All essential information is evident through well-organized work while justifying the solution (5 of 5)<br>☐ Calculations for **Sunken Delivery Truck (A)** and **Crime Scene (B-E)** are complete, correct, and all work was shown using dimensional analysis including units for all numbers throughout calculation (4 total calculations)<br>☐ Calculations for **Suspect #1** are complete, correct, and all work was shown using dimensional analysis including units for all numbers throughout calculation (1 total calculation)<br>☐ Calculations for **Suspect #2** are complete, correct, and all work was shown using dimensional analysis including units for all numbers throughout calculation (2 total calculations)<br>☐ Calculations for **Suspect #3** are complete, correct, and all work was shown using dimensional analysis including units for all numbers throughout calculation (2 total calculations)<br>☐ Calculations for **Suspect #4** are complete, correct, and all work was shown using dimensional analysis including units for all numbers throughout calculation (2 total calculations) | Most essential information is evident through organized work while leading to the solution (4 of 5) | Minimum information is evident through work with a solution present (3 of 4) | Work is extremely unorganized with no solution present (2 or less of 4) | No work shown for this section |

## III. Analysis: Part IV: The Cake Shop Ingredients Analysis—Suspect #3 Special Calculations

| Application | # | wgt | Exemplary (10) | At Standard (8) | In Progress (7) | Still Emerging (6) | No Evaluation (0) |
|---|---|---|---|---|---|---|---|
| Problem Calculations | 2a | ½ | All essential information is evident through well-organized work while justifying the solution (5 of 5) <br>☐ The chemical reaction for the synthesis of vanilla is balanced correctly and correctly written <br>☐ Calculations for the **Limiting Reactant** are complete, correct, and all work was shown including units for all numbers throughout calculation and set up using dimensional analysis <br>☐ Calculations for the **Theoretical Yield of Vanilla** are complete, correct, and all work was shown including units for all numbers throughout calculation and set up using dimensional analysis <br>☐ Calculations for **% Yield** are complete, correct, and all work was shown including units for all numbers throughout calculation <br>☐ **% Composition** for the Excess reagent in the vanilla reaction is shown to determine if any matches to the unknown can be made | Most essential information is evident through organized work while leading to the solution (4 of 5) | Minimum information is evident through work with a solution present (3 of 5) | Work is extremely unorganized with no solution present (1–2 of 5) | No work shown for this section |

## IV. Conclusions

| Application | # | wgt | Exemplary (10) | At Standard (8) | In Progress (7) | Still Emerging (6) | No Evaluation (0) |
|---|---|---|---|---|---|---|---|
| Connecting Ideas | 1d | * | Makes insightful connections between ideas or events that might not be obvious—abstract thinking evident (4 of 4) <br>☐ **Part I conclusion:** All of the 5 chemicals are listed and have realistic reasons for why they were at the crime scene <br>☐ **Part II conclusion:** A connection between the chemicals found on the suspects in Part II is related back to the information from the chemical analysis of the crime scene in Part I <br>☐ **Part III conclusion:** The amounts that were not able to be calculated are correct and are discussed while relating to what having an unknown means for the investigation <br>☐ **Part IV conclusion:** Connections between the unknowns and the crime scene are discussed and a general conclusion can be made about which of the suspects is the lead suspect at this point in the investigation and why | Makes general, logical connections between ideas or events; mostly concrete in nature (3 of 4) | Makes superficial connections between ideas; thinking might be confused or incomplete (2 of 4) | Makes incorrect or no connections between ideas (1 of 4) | No work shown for this section |

## Overall Report Formatting (Extra Credit—5 points)

| Application | # | wgt | |
|---|---|---|---|
| Technology Applications | 1c | * | Technology used is best available and appropriate for the required research, data representation, interpretation, and communication of results. <br>☐ Entire Lab Report is computer generated (5 points); including data tables and calculations typed using the computer |

# The Nuclear Radiation Evidence

## CHEMISTRY CONTENT

- Concentration
- Molarity
- Beer's Law
- Half-Life
- Carbon Dating
- Radioactive Decay
- Nuclear Equations

## NATIONAL SCIENCE EDUCATION STANDARDS ADDRESSED

Content Standard A: Science as Inquiry
Content Standard B: Physical Science
Content Standard E: Science and Technology
Content Standard G: History and Nature of Science

## CASE INFORMATION

Police have learned some additional information about the suspects involved in this case, and their relation to the victim. These details are provided in the Suspect File and have been summarized as follows: The victim, Kirsten K., filed a restraining order against her husband one week prior to her disappearance. Suspect #1, Harold M., was hired by Gladys V., suspect #2, to do some repair work at her lake house. Gladys V. frequently takes walks around the lake when she is staying at the lake house. Since the disappearance of Kirsten K., Suspect #3, Elizabeth G., has seen a decrease in the number of clients at her wedding cake business. Finally, Suspect #4 and the victim's husband, Larry J., was seen leaving an area restaurant with Elizabeth G., suspect #3.

After an extensive search, the body of the victim, Kirsten K., has been located at the crime scene. When the police found the victim, her left ring finger was missing. Police have started to gather evidence from the site where the body was found, including shoe prints, soil samples, and bone fragments. An autopsy on the victim revealed a medical tracer in her body, which should help put a timeline to the murder and also add to the evidence for a cause of death. This performance assessment consists of four parts. In the first part, your students will analyze the soil samples collected at the crime scene and compare them to soil samples from each of the suspects' shoes. In the second part, your students will compare shoe prints found at the crime scene to the shoes from each of the suspects. In the third part, your students will determine the age of some bones found at the crime scene to determine if any of them came from the victim.

Finally, in the fourth part, your students will determine the time of death through the beta decay of the medical tracer found in the victim.

## Part I: The Crime Scene Soil Sample Evidence

In Part I of this assessment, students analyze soil samples from each of the suspects to determine if the concentration of nitrate in the suspect soil sample matches the nitrate amount in the soil from the crime scene. Instead of using real soil, samples of various concentrations are made using iron (III) nitrate. The assessment is designed so that the soil samples from suspect #3, Elizabeth G., and suspect #4, Larry J., match the crime scene samples. However, these could be switched to have students reach a different conclusion. Larry J. was staying at the lake house during the time of the disappearance, so having soil from the crime scene on his shoes would not be suspicious. Elizabeth G.'s presence at the crime scene is more suspicious.

A spectrophotometer, Spec-20, is needed to analyze the soil samples. Students might also use a Vernier Lab Quest with the Spectro-Vis probe attachment to analyze the soil samples. Students will need background knowledge in absorbance and transmittance data collection using Beer's Law so they understand how the data relates to concentration. After placing each of the suspects' soil samples into the Spec-20 and recording the absorbance, students use the Beer's Law calibration curve and plug in absorbance to solve for concentration using the slope of the line. If you are using a different nitrate compound to make the soil, you will have to remake your graph so it fits the compound you are using. If you are using iron (III) nitrate as your soil sample, then you should be able to use the graph provided in the student handout. Students then compare their calculated concentration to the 0.015 M concentration of the crime scene. I usually tell students to choose the suspects with the soil sample concentration closest

to the crime scene concentration because students rarely get exactly 0.015 M when they calculate it.

## Part II: The Shoe Print Evidence

In Part II of the assessment, the suspect's shoe prints are found at the crime scene area, with the exception of Harold M.. Students take each shoe and dust it with a paintbrush and cocoa powder, and then they "walk" it onto the sticky side of the contact paper, as seen in Figure 5.1 Students then stick it to a piece of poster board cut to fit the print to save it for further analysis. After students have made all their prints, they look inside of the evidence envelope to compare all the prints to those prints found at the crime scene. ou will need five different shoes, one for each suspect and one for the victim. Each of the shoes should be tagged using the Forensic Tags provided in Appendix D. The location from which the shoes were collected is up to your discretion. For example, in our scenario, the shoe for Elizabeth G. is found in the trunk of Larry J.'s car, just to provide more evidence that the students can work into their scenarios for the case.

While the shoe print evidence is not always the most conclusive evidence for the case, the students enjoy dusting the shoe prints and comparing them to the police evidence. You may have to remind students that Harold M.'s shoe prints were not at the crime scene, but that does not necessarily mean he was not there. He was doing some work at Gladys V.'s lake house, and he could have worn some of the shoes at the house that were left there by Larry J. from his stay. This section does not involve any of the

*I make a set of prints that serve as the evidence prints to use year after year in the police evidence envelope so that students can compare those to the shoe prints they made.*

## FIGURE 5.1

**SHOE PRINT AND SUPPLIES**

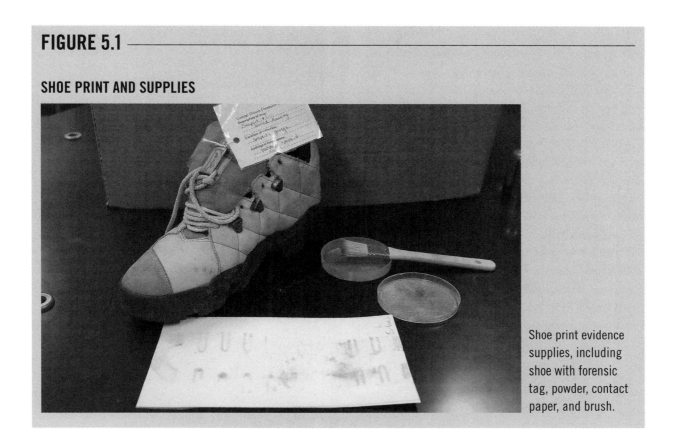

Shoe print evidence supplies, including shoe with forensic tag, powder, contact paper, and brush.

chemistry content that students have learned in this particular unit but does allow them to collect more evidence toward the case.

### Part III: The Bone Age Analysis

In Part III of the assessment, students use half-life calculations to find the age of each of the bones based on the amount of decay, given the amount of parent and daughter isotopes present in each bone. Students find that bone fragments one, two, and four are too old to belong to the victim. Bone fragment number three is the only bone fragment that has not gone through any decay, so it is the only bone fragment that could possibly belong to the victim. Students often need to be reminded that further testing needs to be done to determine that it belongs to the victim, because the age of the bone is not a conclusive test to say the bone belongs to the victim. Students will need background knowledge in determining half-life and will also need to be able to calculate the age of objects using carbon dating. Students do not analyze the bone fragments other than to make visual observations.

> I put pieces of old bone finger fragments from our biology department into four baggies and label them using the forensic tags from Appendix D.

## Part IV: The Medical Tracer Evidence

In Part IV of the assessment, students learn that an autopsy on the victim's body has revealed evidence of a medical tracer. Students need to figure out a timeline to the murder using beta decay. The medical tracer, iodine-131, that was given to the victim has a half-life of 8.04 days. Students learn that the medical tracer is likely the cause of death, and so students work backwards from the isotope, Ba-131, that was found in the victim's body to get an approximate timeline of when she was given the medical tracer. Students should be able to figure out that the medical tracer has gone through three half-lives, which would put the timeline of the murder about 24 days ago. Then students are able to figure out how much medical tracer the victim was given by using the amount that was left in her body. Students will compare the amount that they calculate to the lethal dose amount of 30 g.

In the remaining pages of this chapter, you will find a teacher guide, student handout, suspect file, teacher guide, student lab report example, and grading rubric for Performance Assessment 3: The Nuclear Radiation Evidence. More information about how to use the grading rubric for this and future performance assessments can be found in Appendix B.

The lethal dose amount of 30 g was purely arbitrary and designed solely for the purpose of providing evidence for the students as to how the victim was actually murdered, even though by whom exactly is still to be determined.

# Teacher Guide: *The Nuclear Radiation Evidence*

**Time:** 4–5 days
**Grades:** 11 and 12 (second-year chemistry)

## OBJECTIVES

1. Students will solve a forensics case using their knowledge of chemistry (for performance assessment #3, this includes beer's law calculations, half-life determinations, isotopes, and beta decay).
2. Students will assemble their evidence and present their case at the end of the year.
3. Students will answer four questions:

### Part I

1. Based on the nitrate soil samples, which suspects can be placed at or near the crime scene?

### Part II

1. Based on the shoeprints, which suspects can likely be placed at or near the crime scene?

### Part III

1. Using radioactive dating, which bone fragment could be from the victim?

### Part IV

1. Using half-life calculations, what was the timeframe of the medical tracer and how much was given to the victim?

## PREPARATION

### Part I

You will need a Spec-20 to analyze the soil samples. If this is not available, you could make it more of a qualitative analysis, as the more concentrated the soil sample, the darker the color. You could then have students match the soil samples from the suspects to the soil sample from the crime scene. Students should use the equation for the line given on the graph in their handout to calculate the concentration from the absorbance reading given on the Spec-20. Note that this line is only for the calibration curve for iron (III) nitrate; if another nitrate compound is used, a different calibration curve will have to be made for that sample. When you are making up the samples from each of the suspects, make sure you make the nonmatching suspects lower than 0.015 M because that is on the high end of the trend line, and the Spec-20s can sometimes vary in their outputs of absorbance data.

### Part II

Each shoe needs to be labeled with a forensic tag, which can be found in Appendix D. Make sure to label the locations for each of the shoes so that they fit well with the case and with your desired outcome. These locations are often arbitrary but might help link suspects together. For example, a shoe belonging to Suspect #3, Elizabeth G., might be found in the trunk of Suspect #4, Larry J.'s, car. To make the evidence shoe prints, first brush cocoa powder on the bottom of the shoe. Then, "walk" the shoe on the sticky side of some clear contact paper. Cut out a piece of poster board that is the same size as the contact paper and "preserve" the print by sticking the contact paper to the poster board. Make sure you leave room on the poster board to label the shoe print with the suspect/victim information, or attach a torensic tag to the print.

### Part III

For this activity, students will need a chart of parent and daughter isotopes so that they can match the isotopes to determine how old the bones are for each fragment. They will also need a half-life curve with the number of half-lives on the *x*-axis and the % parent on the *y*-axis. Both of these charts are given to the student in the performance assessment.

### Part IV

No lab preparation needed for this assessment. Students will need a basic understanding of beta decay and half-life to do the calculations in this section.

## QUESTION GUIDELINES

For calculations, formulas, and work, see the student example at the end of the chapter.

### Part I

Suspect #3, Elizabeth G., and Suspect #4, Larry J., had nitrate levels matching those at the crime scene.

### Part II

Suspect #1, Harold M., was not at the crime scene, or he was wearing another suspect's shoes.

### Part III

Bone Fragment #3 could belong to the victim but further testing is needed by the police.

### Part IV

The time frame is 24 days, and the amount of medical tracer found was 34.8 g, which is above the lethal dose of 30 g.

## MATERIALS

### Part I

- Suspect File C
- Student guide
- Spec-20 and nitrate samples from suspects and victim
- Calibration curve

### Part II

- Contact paper
- White poster board
- Large paintbrushes
- Suspect and victim shoes
- Crime scene shoe prints

### Part III

- 4 bone fragments
- Plastic baggies
- Forensic tags

## TEACHER HINTS

In an assessment such as this with multiple parts and equipment needed, I have students rotate each day from one station to another; that way there is less preparation time needed, as you are only making one set of soil samples and one set of shoes, etc.

### Part I

- Students may not get exactly 0.015 M for their concentration but the closer it is to that amount, then the more likely that soil sample matches the crime scene sample.
- Really only two nitrate soil sample solutions need to be made: one that matches the 0.015 M concentration and one that does not. Use the 0.015 M concentration sample only for the suspects that you want to match being at the crime scene.

## Part II

- Students will come up with their own procedure, but here is the correct procedure:
  - o Use large paintbrushes and cocoa powder in petri dishes to dust the bottom of each suspect's shoe.
  - o Lift the print off of the bottom of the shoe with contact paper.
  - o Save the print by sticking the contact paper to a precut piece of white poster board and label.
- Shoes can be purchased from Goodwill stores or ask friends/colleagues for old shoes they are not using anymore.

## Part III

- To make this part of the assessment more exciting for students, I borrow finger bones from the old biology skeletons and place each one in four different baggies labeled with the forensic tags so students can actually see some bone fragments instead of just doing calculations.

Name:_____ Class:_____ Date:_____

# The Case of Kirsten K.:
# *The Nuclear Radiation Evidence*

## PART I: CRIME SCENE SOIL SAMPLE EVIDENCE

### Case Background

Finally, with your help, police were able to find the body of the victim, Kirsten K., and now consider this a murder investigation. When the police found the body, the victim was missing her left ring finger. Police have gathered evidence from the crime scene, including: shoe prints, soil samples, and bones fragments found near the crime scene. A medical tracer was also found in the victim's body which should help put a timeline and a cause of death to the disappearance and the murder of Kirsten K.. Shoes were collected from each of the suspects' homes along with the shoes from the victim's body and taken to the lab to be analyzed for a specific nitrate found in the soil around the crime scene. Police are hoping that this evidence will narrow the suspect list down to those suspects who specifically had this soil nitrate compound in the soil sample on their shoes.

### Purpose

To use the nitrates calibration curve to see which nitrate samples from the suspects match the crime scene sample.

### Procedure

1. Test the nitrate soil samples taken from each suspect's shoe and from the crime scene.
2. Set the Spec-20 to the wavelength of maximum absorbance = 400 nm.
3. Record results of absorbance from the Spec-20 for each of the 4 samples from each of the 4 suspects in a data table in the data section.

### Materials

- Spec-20 and supplies
- Nitrate samples from suspects #1–4 and victim
- Calibration curve

### Data
### TABLE 1

**CONCENTRATION OF CRIME SCENE SAMPLE**

| Location of Sample | Concentration (M) |
|---|---|
| Crime Scene | 0.015M |

Create a data table to record the absorbance from each of the suspect samples in the data table format.

# ANALYSIS: CALCULATIONS

Police need the concentration for each of the four suspect samples to prove the match since the crime scene soil nitrate sample is given as a concentration in the data section.

Use the graph given below and/or the equation for the slope of the line to extrapolate and/or calculate the concentration for each of the suspect samples.

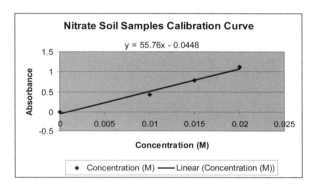

Calculations (If the equation for the slope of the line was used to find concentration, show calculations below.)

# PART II: THE SHOE PRINT EVIDENCE

## Background Information

Shoe prints are found at the scene of a crime. The design of the shoe can often allow police to link a particular shoe print with a given shoe type. While the shoe and owner cannot directly be linked in this manner, determining which suspects have similar shoes to the prints found at the crime scene may provide further evidence linking the suspects to the victim.

## Purpose

To record evidence for the shoe prints made by each of the suspects' shoes and the victim's shoes to see if they match the prints found at the crime scene. Crime scene prints are in the sealed envelope marked with an evidence tag. ONLY view the evidence prints after making impressions of each of the suspect's shoes.

## Procedure

Record the procedure in a numbered list of steps for recording the shoe print evidence.

_____
_____
_____
_____
_____
_____
_____
_____

## Conclusion

Which of the suspects were present at the crime scene? How did the Spec-20 absorbance data help determine the suspects who were or were not present? Who are the lead suspects at this time and why?

_____
_____
_____
_____
_____

## Materials

List the materials used to complete the procedure.

_____
_____
_____

### Data

1. Create a data table to compare any quantitative and/or qualitative data from the shoe prints of the suspects and victim to those found at the crime scene.

2. Check the evidence file for shoe prints that were found at the crime scene and record your findings in the data table above **OR** create a new table to identify any matches.

### Conclusion

What connections can be made, if any, between the crime scene shoe prints and the shoe prints from the suspects and victim? Does this help to narrow the suspect list? If so, how? If not, why not?

_____
_____
_____
_____
_____
_____

## PART III: THE BONE AGE EVIDENCE

### Background Information

Since discovering that the victim was missing her left ring finger, police have decided to scan the area, specifically the lake to find it. Police have found four total pieces of bone that they believe could be the finger of the victim. The police need to find out which piece of bone, if any, could belong to the victim for further testing.

### Purpose

To determine which bone fragment(s) could have possibly belonged to the victim by using radioactive isotope dating.

*Data*
# TABLE 1

**BONE FRAGMENT #1**

| ISOTOPES PRESENT | AMOUNT (MOLES) |
|---|---|
| Calcium-40 | 0.561 |
| Iron-56 | 0.003 |
| Carbon-14 | 5.669 |
| Rhodium-103 | 9.321 |
| Nitrogen-14 | 6.003 |
| Scandium-45 | 1.056 |

# TABLE 2

**BONE FRAGMENT #2**

| ISOTOPES PRESENT | AMOUNT (MOLES) |
|---|---|
| Uranium-235 | 9.632 |
| Nitrogen-14 | 3.000 |
| Carbon-14 | 1.575 |
| Lead-206 | 2.595 |
| Rubidium-87 | 7.667 |
| Scandium-45 | 8.531 |

# TABLE 3

**BONE FRAGMENT #3**

| ISOTOPES PRESENT | AMOUNT (MOLES) |
|---|---|
| Lead-208 | 3.250 |
| Nitrogen-14 | 0.000 |
| Argon-40 | 0.001 |
| Scandium-45 | 1.376 |
| Uranium-235 | 11.125 |
| Carbon-14 | 0.008 |

# TABLE 4

**BONE FRAGMENT #4**

| ISOTOPES PRESENT | AMOUNT (MOLES) |
|---|---|
| Carbon-14 | 5.320 |
| Iron-56 | 1.500 |
| Potassium-40 | 2.678 |
| Thorium-232 | 9.381 |
| Lead-206 | 1.333 |
| Nitrogen-14 | 2.054 |

## Analysis: Graphing

Identify the percentage of parent and daughter isotopes for each sample on the half-life curve provided:

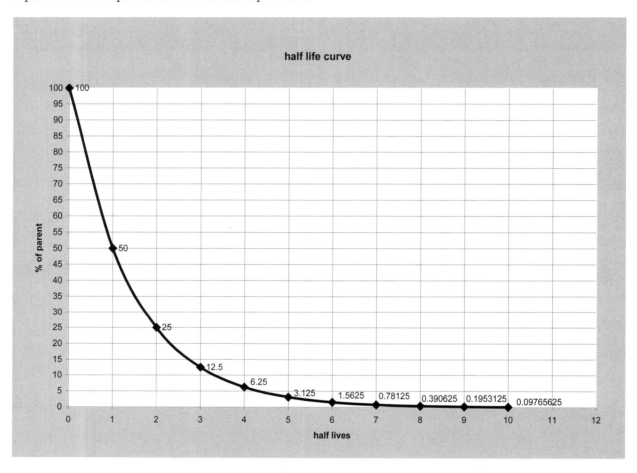

_____

| PARENT ISOTOPES | DAUGHTER ISOTOPES | HALF-LIFE OF PARENT (YEARS) | EFFECTIVE DATING RANGE (YEARS) | MINERALS AND OTHER MATERIALS THAT CAN BE DATED |
|---|---|---|---|---|
| Uranium-238 Uranium-235 Thorium-232 | Lead-206 Lead-207 Lead-208 | 4.5 billion 710 million 14 billion | 10 million–4.5 billion | Zircon, uraninite, and pitchlende |
| Potassium-40 | Argon-40 Calcium-40 | 1.3 billion | 100,000–4.6 billion | Muscovite, biotite, hornblende, whole volcanic rock |
| Rubidium-87 | Strotium-87 | 47 billion | 10 million–4.6 billion | Muscovite, biotite, potassium-feldspar, whole metamorphic or igneous rock |
| Carbon-14 | Nitrogen-14 | 5,730 | 100–50,000 | Wood, charcoal, peat, grain, and other plant material; bone, tissue, and other animal material; cloth, shell, ground-water, ocean water, and glacier ice |

## Analysis: Calculations

Show calculations for each of the bone fragments to prove the age and whether or not this fragment belongs to the victim:

Bone Fragment #1

Bone Fragment #2

Bone Fragment #3

Bone Fragment #4

## CONCLUSION

Which of the bone fragments, if any, belongs to the victim? How can the others be ruled out? Is this test conclusive? Why or why not?

_____
_____
_____
_____
_____
_____
_____
_____
_____
_____

## PART IV: THE MEDICAL TRACER EVIDENCE

### Background Information

After further testing was done on the finger of the victim, it was found that the victim had the medical tracer iodine-131, in her system. Iodine-131 is known to have a half-life of 8.04 days and goes through beta decay. When the bone marrow from the victim's finger was tested, it was found to have the isotope $^{131}_{56}Ba$.

## PURPOSE

To determine the time frame in which the murder took place by figuring out how long ago the body was exposed to the medical tracer.

## ANALYSIS: CALCULATIONS

Show all work for the reverse decay pattern for the $^{131}_{56}Ba$.

Using the time frame determined from the medical tracer data, calculate the amount of medical tracer (I-131) that was given to the victim prior to her death if 4.35 g was calculated to remain in the body when it was found by police. The lethal dose of medical tracer is 30.0 g.

### Conclusion

1. What is the time frame of the murder, starting from the victim's reported disappearance up to the murder?

_____
_____
_____
_____
_____
_____

2. Who are the lead suspects at this point? Don't forget to look at the suspect files. Can you determine any motives of any of the prime suspects at this point?

_____
_____
_____
_____
_____
_____
_____
_____

# SUSPECT FILE C

### Victim: Kirsten K.

- Filed for a restraining order against her husband just a week before her disappearance

### Suspect #1: Harold M.

- Was hired by Gladys V. to do some repair work at her lake house

### Suspect #2: Gladys V.

- Enjoys taking walks around the lake when she is staying at her lake house

### Suspect #3: Elizabeth G.

- Has shown a decrease in number of clients for her wedding cake business since the disappearance of Kirsten K.

### Suspect #4: Larry J.

- Recently was seen leaving a restaurant in the area with Elizabeth G.

Name:_____ Class:_____ Date:_____

# Student Lab Report Example:
# *The Nuclear Radiation Evidence*

## I. INTRODUCTION

### A) Background Information

From the previous information found in the case of Kirsten K., the police were able to find her body, but unfortunately they were too late, as she was found dead. Nevertheless, when the police found Kirsten's body, which happened to be not far from the crime scene analyzed from before, they discovered that the victim was missing her left ring finger. Now, the police have gathered evidence from the crime scene, which includes shoe prints, soil samples, and bone fragments found near the scene. According to the autopsy, a medical tracer was also found in the victim's body which will help the police and the forensic scientists put a timeline on the disappearance and the murder of Kirsten K. Shoes were collected from each suspects' home along with the shoes from the victim's body and taken to a lab. The shoes were analyzed for a specific nitrate found in the soil at the crime scene, and police are hoping that this evidence will shorten the suspect list down. While the shoes were being analyzed for nitrates, the police were also searching for shoeprints around the crime scene that would provide further evidence to rule out or help convict specific suspects for being at the crime scene. Four pieces of bone were also found at the crime scene near the body. Police believe they could belong to the victim, specifically bones from the missing left ring finger. Lastly, after testing the body, the autopsy revealed a medical tracer within the body. By using the amount that is left in the body it will help police determine the timeline associated with the death of the victim, Kirsten K.

### B) Purpose

The purpose is to determine the most likely suspects based on the new evidence collected from the soil samples, shoe prints, bone fragments, and medical tracer left in the body.

## II. DATA

### *Part I: The Crime Scene Soil Sample Evidence*
## TABLE 1

SOIL SAMPLE ABSORBANCE CHART

| Suspects | Location | Absorbance | Wavelength of Maximum Absorbance | Match (Yes or No) |
|---|---|---|---|---|
| 1 | Harold M.'s Shoe | 0.457 | 400 | No |
| 2 | Gladys V.'s Shoe | 0.399 | 400 | No |
| 3 | Elizabeth G.'s Shoe | 0.855 | 400 | Yes |
| 4 | Larry J.'s Shoe | 0.758 | 400 | Yes |

### *Part II: The Shoe Print Evidence*
## TABLE 2

LOOK AND SIZE SHOE CHART

| Shoe | Quantitative (Size) | Qualitative (style) | Where Found | Match (Yes or No) |
|---|---|---|---|---|
| Victim: Kirsten K. | 9.5 | Black Velcro Shoe | At the crime scene | Yes-C |
| Suspect #1: Harold M. | 13 | Work Boot | In the garage of his house | No |
| Suspect #2: Gladys V. | 9.5 | Tan Suede Shoe | Outside the back door of her lake house | Yes-B |
| Suspect #3: Elizabeth G. | 8.5 | Brown Clog (slip-on) | In the trunk of Larry Jensen's car | Yes-A |
| Suspect #4: Larry J. | 11.5 | Golf Shoe | In trunk of his car | Yes-D |

# III. ANALYSIS: CALCULATIONS

## Part I: The Crime Scene Soil Sample Evidence
### CALCULATIONS FOR ABSORBANCE CONCENTRATION CHARTS

| Location of Sample | Concentration (M) | Equation for Slope of Line | Match (Yes or No) |
|---|---|---|---|
| Crime Scene Soil Sample | 0.015 M | $y = 55.76x - 0.0448$ | |
| Suspect #1: Harold M. | 0.009 M | $0.457 = 55.76x - 0.0448$ | No |
| Suspect #2: Gladys V. | 0.008 M | $0.399 = 55.76x - 0.0448$ | No |
| Suspect #3: Elizabeth G. | 0.016 M | $0.855 = 55.76x - 0.0448$ | Yes |
| Suspect #4: Larry J. | 0.014 M | $0.758 = 55.76x - 0.0448$ | Yes |

## Part III: The Bone Age Analysis
### CALCULATIONS FOR THE AGE OF THE BONE FRAGMENTS

| Bone Fragment # | Amount of Parent and Daughter Isotopes | Part (Parent) x 100 Whole (Parent + Daughter) = % Parent | # of half-lives | Age of Object | Victim's (Yes or No) |
|---|---|---|---|---|---|
| 1 | Carbon-14 = 5.669 moles  Nitrogen-14 = 6.003 moles | $\dfrac{5.669}{11.672} \times 100 = 48.6\%$ | 1 half-life | $\dfrac{1\ \text{half-life}}{} \mid \dfrac{5730\ \text{years}}{1\ \text{half-life}}$ = 5730 years | No, too old |
| 2 | Carbon-14 = 1.575 moles  Nitrogen-14 = 3.000 moles | $\dfrac{1.575}{4.575} \times 100 = 34.4\%$ | 1.6 half-life | $\dfrac{1.6\ \text{half-life}}{} \mid \dfrac{5730\ \text{years}}{1\ \text{half-life}}$ = 9168 years | No, too old |
| 3 | Carbon-14 = 0.008 moles  Nitrogen-14 = 0.000 moles | $\dfrac{0.008}{0.008} \times 100 = 100\%$ | 0 half-lives | $\dfrac{0\ \text{half-life}}{} \mid \dfrac{5730\ \text{years}}{1\ \text{half-life}}$ = 0 years | Yes, could belong to victim |
| 4 | Carbon-14 = 5.320 moles  Nitrogen-14 = 2.054 moles | $\dfrac{5.320}{7.374} \times 100 = 72\%$ | 0.5 half-lives | $\dfrac{0.5\ \text{half-life}}{} \mid \dfrac{5730\ \text{years}}{1\ \text{half-life}}$ = 2865 years | No, too old |

## Part IV: The Medical Tracer Evidence
### Calculations for the reverse decay pattern for the $^{131}_{56}$Ba

$$^{131}_{56}\text{Ba} \leftarrow\ ^{131}_{55}\text{Cs} \leftarrow\ ^{131}_{54}\text{Xe} \leftarrow\ ^{131}_{53}\text{I}$$

Each decay for the medical tracer takes 8.04 days. The medical tracer underwent 3 beta decays to become the isotope that was found within the victim, Kirsten K.

$$\frac{3 \text{ decays}}{} \quad \Big| \quad \frac{8.04 \text{ days}}{1 \text{ decay}} = 24.12 \text{ days ago the medical tracer was given to the victim}$$

**Calculations for the amount of medical tracer given to the victim**

### Option #1: Natural Log Equation

ln (Nt/No) = kt
ln = natural log
Nt = amount of isotope at time t
No = original amount
k = half life constant; k = 0.693/half life
t = time

ln (4.35/No) = (0.693/8.04)24.12
(4.35/No) = e^2.079
4.35/No = 1.25053
No = 34.8 g
34.8 g is above the lethal dose amount which means Kirsten K. was abducted several months ago but was not murdered until she was given the excess of medical tracer

OR

### Option #2: Work backward with the decay calculations

4.35 g (3 decays) → 8.70 g (2 decays) → 17.40 g (1 decay) → 34.80 g (0 decays)

***original amount of medical tracer given to victim, which is over the lethal dose amount

# CONCLUSION

## Part I: The Crime Scene Soil Sample Evidence

Which of the suspects were present at the crime scene? How did the Spec-20 absorbance data help determine the suspects who were or were not present? Who are the lead suspects at this time and why?

The lead suspects at this point in the investigation are Elizabeth G. and Larry J. The crime scene soil sample has a nitrate concentration of 0.015 M and the two suspects had the closest nitrate soil concentration match to that with a 0.016 M and 0.014 M. Larry J. was renting out the lake house owned by Gladys V. the week that Kirsten went missing, so he was around the lake and the crime scene at some point to have the matching soil on his shoes. But the fact that Elizabeth G. was at the crime scene is more suspicious, especially since she was recently seen leaving a restaurant in the area with Larry J. Because there was a restraining order filed against Larry J., it may indicate that his relationship with the victim, Kirsten K., was not going well and Elizabeth G. may have been the reason. People may be talking in the community about the murder and Elizabeth G.'s connection to it because her wedding cake business has declined in the last few months since Kirsten's disappearance and the sunken delivery truck incident.

## Part II: The Shoe Print Evidence

What connections can be made if any between the crime scene shoe prints and the shoe prints from the suspects and victim? Does this help to narrow the suspect list? If so, how? If not, why not?

The police have discovered that some of the footprints taken as samples from the suspects were in fact found at the crime scene. Harold M.'s footprint was the only one not sighted at the scene, which indicated to the police very clearly that he was not at the location of where the victim Kirsten K. disappeared. This means that the only suspects left to further investigate are Gladys V. who is an elderly woman that likes to take walks at the location where the victim's body was found. Gladys V. also owns a lake house on Clinton Lake so it would make sense that her footprints would be around the area. Elizabeth G. who was the employer of the victim has no reason to be at the most recent crime scene. The fact that the victim's left ring finger was missing may indicate that Elizabeth G. was jealous of the victim and Larry's relationship as husband and wife and was trying to send a message by cutting off the finger that would normally have a wedding ring on it. Larry J.'s shoe prints were also found at the crime scene, which is odd, unless he was going to the lake house to meet with Gladys V. to buy drugs, since Gladys V. had cocaine on her when last tested and Larry J. has been convicted of drug use in the past. Also, Larry J. could have been the one to cut off the left ring finger to get his wedding ring back, since the victim had filed a restraining order against him recently.

## Part III: The Bone Age Analysis

Which of the bone fragments, if any, belongs to the victim? How can the others be ruled out? Is this test conclusive? Why or why not?

So when it comes to the bone fragments found at the crime scene by the police, they should investigate the third bone fragment further because the other fragments found at the crime scene have been there for over 2,000 years and bone fragment three has not decayed yet at all. The bone fragments all have Carbon-14 in them and decay to the daughter isotope of nitrogen-14. Bone Fragment #3 hasn't even begun to decay because it shows 0.000 moles of nitrogen-14 present in the bone. The test is not conclusive because the bone may not necessarily belong to Kirsten just because it is not as old as the other bone fragments found in the area.

## *Part IV: The Medical Tracer Evidence*

What is the time frame of the murder, starting from the victim's reported disappearance up to the murder? Who are the lead suspects at this point? Don't forget to look at the suspect files. Can you determine any motives of any of the prime suspects at this point?

Now the medical tracer found in the victim's body can create a time frame of when the victim went missing to when she was murdered. Because the half-life of the medical tracer is known, the time frame from the disappearance of Kirsten K. that happened several months ago can now be related to her actual murder that happened 24 days ago according to the medical tracer decay data. The medical tracer, iodine-131, has a half-life of 8.04 days and it was determined that the tracer went through 3 half-lives after being given to the victim to murder her. The amount of medical tracer left in the victim at the time the body was found to be 4.35 g. By working backward with the decay of the tracer, the original amount of the medical tracer given to the victim was calculated to be 34.8 g, which is over the lethal dose of 30 g.

The evidence from the case of Kirsten K. so far leads police to start questioning Larry and Elizabeth because the soil from their shoes matches the soil from the crime scene, their shoes were at the crime scene, and the left ring finger is missing which is a finger that would normally have the wedding ring on it. Both lead suspects were seen leaving a local restaurant together, which is odd even, especially at a time when Larry J.'s wife has been missing. The suspects need to be questioned about the possible romantic relationship forming between the two of them and about the reasons that they were around the Clinton Lake area.

# GRADING RUBRIC C

Name _____    Score _____ /40 _____    % Grade _____

## I. Introduction

| Application | # | wgt | Exemplary (10) | At Standard (8) | In Progress (7) | Still Emerging (6) | No Evaluation (0) |
|---|---|---|---|---|---|---|---|
| Defining Problems | 1a | * | Definition of problem or issue reflects a broad, insightful view (4 of 4) <br> ☐ **Background Information** for Part I is summarized in your own words <br> ☐ **Background Information** for Part II is summarized in your own words <br> ☐ **Background Information** for Part III is summarized in your own words <br> ☐ **Background Information** for Part IV is summarized in your own words | Definition of problem or issue is reasonable and concise (3 of 4) | Definition of problem has aspects that are vague or incomplete (2 of 4) | Overall definition of problem is vague or unreasonable (1 of 4) | No work shown for this section |

## II. Data

| Application | # | wgt | Exemplary (10) | At Standard (8) | In Progress (7) | Still Emerging (6) | No Evaluation (0) |
|---|---|---|---|---|---|---|---|
| Interpreting Models | 1b | * | Interprets visuals or models at a complex level (4 of 4) <br> ☐ Data table for Part I: Nitrate Soil is constructed to show the suspect # and the absorbance for that sample with units and labels where needed <br> ☐ Data table for Part II: Shoeprint shows qualitative and/or quantitative data with units and labels where needed <br> ☐ Data table for Part II: Shoeprint shows a match with the evidence envelope shoeprints (Evidence A–D) <br> ☐ Correct **titles** are used for all data tables required for this assessment | Interprets visuals or models at a general level (3 of 4) | Interpretation of visuals or models contains errors that restrict understanding (2 of 4) | Shows fundamental errors in use and understanding of visuals (1 of 4) | No work turned in for this section |

## III. Analysis-No Graph Needed
## III. Analysis-Calculations

| Application | # | wgt | Exemplary (10) | At Standard (8) | In Progress (7) | Still Emerging (6) | No Evaluation (0) |
|---|---|---|---|---|---|---|---|
| Problem Calculations | 2a | * | All essential information is evident through well-organized work while justifying the solution (4 of 4)<br>□ Two Calculations using the equation for the slope of the line for **Part I: Nitrate Soil are shown** for any concentrations that match the crime scene and are complete, correct, and ALL WORK is included along with units for all numbers throughout calculation<br>□ Three calculations are shown for **Part III: Bone Fragments** for finding the age of the bone fragments and are complete, correct, and ALL WORK is included along with units for all numbers throughout the calculation<br>□ Calculations for **Part IV: Medical Tracer** for the reverse decay of the Barium isotope are shown to calculate the time frame for the exposure of the victim to the medical tracer<br>□ Calculations for **Part IV: Medical Tracer** for the amount of medical tracer the victim was originally exposed to is complete, correct, and ALL WORK is included along with units for all numbers throughout the calculation. | Most essential information is evident through organized work while leading to the solution (3 of 4) | Minimum information is evident through work with a solution present (2 of 4) | Work is extremely unorganized with no solution present (1 of 4) | No work shown for this section |

## IV. Conclusions

| Application | # | wgt | Exemplary (10) | At Standard (8) | In Progress (7) | Still Emerging (6) | No Evaluation (0) |
|---|---|---|---|---|---|---|---|
| Connecting Ideas | 1d | * | Makes insightful connections between ideas or events that might not be obvious—abstract thinking evident (4 of 4)<br>□ **Part I conclusion:** Which of the suspects were at the crime scene and how does the Spec-20/labquest data help prove this?<br>□ **Part II conclusion:** What connections can be made between the crime scene shoeprints and those shoeprints of the suspects?<br>□ **Part III conclusion:** Which of the bone fragments must belong to the victim and why? How can the other bone fragments be ruled out for belonging to the victim?<br>□ **Part IV conclusion:** How does the medical tracer data help put a time frame together for the murder and what is the time frame? Who are the lead suspects at this point? Is there a motive yet? | Makes general, logical connections between ideas or events; mostly concrete in nature (3 of 4) | Makes superficial connections between ideas; thinking might be confused or incomplete (2 of 4) | Makes incorrect or no connections between ideas (1 of 4) | No work shown for this section |

## Overall Report Formatting (Extra Credit—5 points)

| Application | # | wgt | |
|---|---|---|---|
| Technology Applications | 1c | * | Technology used is best available and appropriate for the required research, data representation, interpretation, and communication of results.<br>□ Entire Lab Report is computer generated (5 points); including data tables and calculations typed using the computer |

# The Weapon Analysis Evidence

## CHEMISTRY CONTENT

- Electrochemistry
- Redox Reactions
- Titrations
- Molarity
- Stoichiometry
- pH
- Acids and Bases

## NATIONAL SCIENCE EDUCATION STANDARDS ADDRESSED

Content Standard A: Science as Inquiry
Content Standard B: Physical Science
Content Standard G: History and Nature of Science

## CASE INFORMATION

Police have learned some additional information about the suspects involved in this case, and their relationship to the victim. These details are provided in the Suspect File and have been summarized as follows: Suspect #1, Harold M., started his own plumbing business and is a licensed gun owner. Gladys V., suspect #2, has just received the Hunters Unlimited Alumni Volunteer Award and has a deer permit issued for the current hunting season. Elizabeth G., Suspect #3, recently eloped in Las Vegas with her longtime boyfriend, and made her own wedding cake for the occasion. The body of Larry J., suspect #4 and the victim's husband, was found in the basement of Gladys V.'s lake house. Finally, a new suspect #5, Gerald V., has entered the picture. He is the son of Gladys, also has a deer permit for the current season, and lives with Gladys in the lake house.

When we were making this yearlong case, we got to the point where we felt like we had exhausted most of the options for the murder of Kirsten. Worried that the students might become bored and lose interest in the case, we decided that an additional murder, or second victim, would help to finish out the last two units of the year. Thus, students learn that suspect #4, Larry J., who was the original victim's husband, has been murdered. As a result, introducing this particular assessment is done a little bit differently than the previous assessments. I invite our school resource officer, or police officer, to interrupt my class to let us know there has been a new murder in the case of Kirsten K.

*If you don't have a police officer on your school campus, you could invite your principal or a department colleague to interrupt your class and tell you that you have a phone call, then come back to class and make the announcement that Larry J. has been murdered.*

Not only did we need to introduce a new murder, but we also had to introduce a new suspect, Gerald V., who is Gladys's son. We felt that at this point we needed to add a twist to the plot. As soon as our school police officer walks into the room to announce that there has been a new murder, students often laugh; however, they do appreciate our attempt to make this a "real life" case for them. After the police officer announces Larry J.'s murder, he goes through a script that we developed that foreshadows the parts of the assessment the students are about to complete. He discusses the importance of analyzing fingerprints at a crime scene and goes through how to dust them. He also discusses ballistics and bullet analysis, gunshot residue, and blood stains. By having someone else introduce this particular assessment, it immediately gains the students' interest and gives them a renewed insight into solving this new murder case.

## Part I: The Fingerprint Analysis

This part of the assessment is separated and given to the students immediately after the police officer leaves the classroom, after introducing the new case. Students do not know about the new suspect at the time that they begin analyzing the fingerprint evidence.

Students learn that Larry J. has been found murdered in Gladys V.'s basement with bullet wounds to the chest. Police have recovered two guns, one with an aluminum foil-covered handle and another gun that was made out of copper. Police have found fingerprints on both guns and want students to analyze the prints to see if they match any of the current suspects. From their analysis, students discover an unknown fingerprint on each of the two different gun handles. At this point, students receive the new suspect list for this assessment, Suspect List D, which links the fingerprints to a new suspect #5, Gerald V.

When students are analyzing the fingerprints from the aluminum and copper gun handles, an evidence folder of all the suspects' fingerprints is available for students to use to compare with the gun handle fingerprints. An example of one of these fingerprint files can be seen in Figure 6.1. I recommend that students try to match the fingerprints first to the evidence file before they try to dust them because students often ruin the prints as they try to dust and preserve them, and then are unable to match them. Details on how the students dust for the fingerprints can be found in the student assessment handout. To make the fingerprints that I need to be on the gun handles each year, I try to use fingerprints that are readily available. For example, I use my own fingerprints for Gladys's fingerprints. This way, I don't have to make a new evidence sheet each year if I use someone else's fingerprints. Larry J., Gladys V., and Gerald V. are the owners of the three prints found on each of the gun handles. I use actual police fingerprinting paperwork for each of the suspect's prints, and then I just make enough copies so that each group has one. That way, all students are analyzing fingerprints at the same time. Each group also receives a copy of each gun handle with prints. I use aluminum foil pieces and copper foil pieces to represent each gun handle.

## FIGURE 6.1

### FINGERPRINT SAMPLE

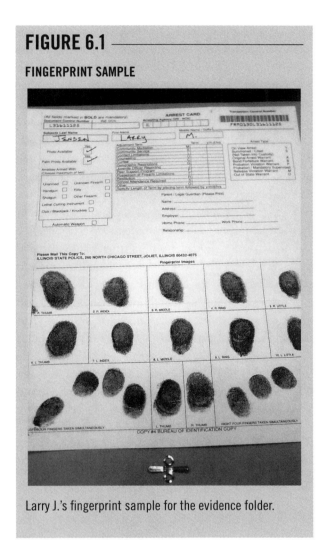

Larry J.'s fingerprint sample for the evidence folder.

These prints must be made each year and then labeled in baggies with a forensics tag. Also, if you have multiple classes, you will need multiple sets of fingerprints on the aluminum and copper foils because the prints cannot be reused once the students have dusted for them.

## *Part II: Gun and Bullet Matching*

In Part II of the assessment, the students try to match the two types of guns with the aluminum and copper handles with the two types of bullets found at the crime scene. These bullets were made from silver and zinc. Using electrochemistry concepts, students can determine which bullet goes with which gun by analyzing the half reactions and cell potentials for each of the four metals and determining which combination will provide the correct range of potential difference. The electrical cell potential difference for

this assessment was arbitrarily chosen to be between 0 and +1.0 Volts for the gun and bullet to be a match. While the potential difference and its relationship to the gun and bullet is not realistic, the process helps students with their understanding of electrochemistry and allows them to gather more evidence in the case of the murder of Larry J. Students will also need to consider whose fingerprints are on each gun and which bullet came from which gun in order to determine which gun belonged to Larry J. and which gun belonged to the V. family. Although Larry J., Gerald V., and Gladys V.'s fingerprints were all found on the guns involved in the murder, a gunshot residue test will give more conclusive evidence of who actually shot the guns.

## *Part III: Gunshot Residue*

In Part III of the assessment, students perform five titration labs to test each of the suspects for gunshot residue. If students calculate the acid concentration to be higher than 0.15 M, then a positive match exists. I usually make two acid solutions, one that is higher than 0.15 M and one that is lower than 0.15 M. Then I use the higher concentration solution for the suspects that I want to be positive for gunshot residue, in this case it is Larry J. and Gerald V. Students should have done titrations before, using base in the buret and various indicators to show the color change when the endpoint is reached. Although time constraints may limit the number of trials students are able to conduct, they are encouraged to use the data of other groups and take the average in order to achieve the best results.

## Part IV: Blood Stain Analysis

In Part IV of the assessment, students use pH to determine whether or not the stains found on each suspect are blood, and if so, whose blood. There is no lab work with this particular part of the assessment but it does give students some important evidence about the murders of Kirsten K. and Larry J. By looking at the blood evidence, both Larry J. and Kirsten K.'s blood is found on Gerald V., whereas Gerald V. and Larry J.'s blood is found on Larry J. Gladys V. has Gerald V.'s blood on her, which strengthens Gladys V.'s potential involvement in Larry J.'s murder. In addition to the blood stains, students find two other stains on Harold M. and Elizabeth G. and are asked to consider different possibilities for the identity of those stains based on the suspects' jobs. Students should find that Harold M. has some type of basic stain on him, which could be some kind of cleaning supply, given his occupation as a plumber. Students should also find that Elizabeth G. has an acidic stain on her, possibly from the production of vanilla in her cake shop since glyoxylic acid is an ingredient. While we did not include kinetics and equilibrium topics in this assessment, these topics could be included in this section. For example, this part could be extended to give students a $K_a$ value for a specific dissociation of a strong or a weak acid reaction, and then students could solve for a pH value, which they would then apply to the blood-matching section in Part IV.

In the remaining pages of this chapter, you will find a teacher guide, student handout, suspect file, student lab report example, and grading rubric for Performance Assessment 4: The Weapon Analysis Evidence. More information about how to use the grading rubric for this and future performance assessments can be found in Appendix B.

# Teacher Guide:
# *The Weapon Analysis Evidence*

**Time:** 4–5 days
**Grades:** 11 and 12 (second-year chemistry)

## OBJECTIVES

1.  Students will solve a forensics case using their knowledge of chemistry (for performance assessment #4, this includes half-reactions, voltaic cells, activity series, acid/base chemistry, and titrations).
2.  Students will assemble their evidence and present their case at the end of the year.
3.  Students will answer seven questions:

### Part I

1.  Which suspects are potential matches to the fingerprints found on the gun with the aluminum foil handle?
2.  Which suspects are potential matches to the fingerprints found on the gun with the copper handle?

### Part II

1.  Which bullet type was matched to each gun and what evidence proves this?

### Part III

1.  Which suspects were positive matches for gunshot residue? Which were negative matches?

### Part IV

1.  Which of the suspects and/or victims had stains on their clothing that fell into the pH range of blood?

2.  Why might Suspect #1, Harold M., have had a basic stain on his clothing and Suspect #3, Elizabeth G., have had an acidic stain? You may have to look back at previous assessments and/or suspect files.
3.  Which of the suspects/victims matched the blood stains?

## PREPARATION

### Part I

You will need pieces of copper foil and aluminum foil to represent the gun handles. Place one of each sample into a baggie for each group to analyze, labeling them with a forensic tag. Make sure that the copper foil contains the fingerprints for Gladys V. and Gerald V. The aluminum foil should contain the fingerprints for Larry J. and Gerald V. You will also need to make fingerprint charts for each suspect so that students can compare the fingerprints on the gun handles to the fingerprint charts. Only one chart needs to be made (you will find a blank form at the end of this teacher guide); you can provide copies for each group to use as a comparison. Any fingerprints can be used for Harold M. and Elizabeth G. because you will not need those prints again until you need to make new fingerprint charts. However, for the prints of Gladys V., Gerald V., and Larry J., make sure you use fingerprints from someone who is available to make fresh prints every year since you will need to re-make the copper and aluminum foil samples each year.

### Part II

In order to do the half-reaction calculations, students will need a half-reaction chart to look up the cell potentials for each of the four metal half reactions. These charts are readily available in most advanced chemistry textbooks.

### Part III

For this activity, you will need to prepare two acidic solutions, likely HCl. One of these solutions needs to be a high concentration (0.2 M or higher), and the other needs to be a low concentration (0.05 M). There needs to be a definite difference in concentrations in order for the students to determine who does and does not test positive for gunshot residue.

### Part IV

No lab preparation needed for this assessment. Students will need an understanding of how to calculate pH from the $[H_3O^+]$ and $[OH^-]$ concentrations to complete the calculations portion of this activity.

## QUESTION GUIDELINES

For calculations, formulas, and work, see the student example at the end of the chapter.

### Part I

1. Aluminum foil prints belong to Suspect #4: Larry J. and also an Unknown (later introduced in Suspect File D as Suspect #5: Gerald V.).
2. Copper handle prints belong to Suspect #2: Gladys V. and also an Unknown (later introduced in Suspect File D as Suspect #5: Gerald V.).

### Part II

1. Aluminum handle gun had the zinc bullet; copper handle gun had the silver bullet.
2. Aluminum handle gun belongs to Larry J.; copper handle gun belongs to Gerald V. and Gladys V.

### Part III

1. Suspects Gladys V. and Gerald V. and victim Larry J. were positive for gunshot residue. Suspects Harold M. and Elizabeth G. were negative for gunshot residue.

### Part IV

1. Victims Kirsten K. and Larry J. and Suspects Gladys V. and Gerald V. all had clothing that tested positive for blood stains.
2. Harold M. was positive for a basic stain because he is a plumber and works with basic cleaners. Elizabeth G. was positive for an acidic stain because she uses glyoxylic acid when making vanilla for her cakes, as learned in the second performance assessment *(See Chapter 4: The Chemical Evidence)*.
3. Kirsten K.'s blood stains were her own blood. Larry J.'s blood stains were both his own blood and the blood of Gerald V.. Gerald V.'s blood stains included his own blood, the blood of Kirsten K., and the blood of Larry J.. Gladys V.'s blood stains included the blood of Gerald V.

## MATERIALS

### Part I

- Suspect File D
- Student guide
- Copper foil pieces
- Aluminum foil pieces
- Fingerprint evidence charts
- Powder/brushes/clear tape/white and black paper

### Part IV

- Titration setups per lab group
- 0.1 M NaOH
- HCl samples for each suspect

## TEACHER HINTS

### Introduction to the Assessment

- Included at the end of this teacher guide is the script used with the school police officer. If you do not have a police officer at your school, you could call the county coroner, a defense lawyer, or a local forensic scientist to come in and speak.
- DO NOT HAND OUT THE SUSPECT FILE WITH THIS ASSESSMENT! You will want to hand out the fingerprint assessment Part I prior to handing out the rest of the assessment parts (II–IV) and suspect file becauase a new suspect will be introduced after Part I is complete.

### Part I

- For the recurring fingerprints for the gun handles (Larry J., Gerald V., and Gladys V.), I use prints that are readily available. For example, I use my own prints for Gladys and my husband's prints for Gerald V.. A school administrator provides the prints for Larry J. It doesn't matter who you choose, as long as they can provide prints every year. Otherwise, you will have to remake the fingerprint charts each year.
- Fingerprints need to be made as close to using them as possible. Otherwise, they get smudged if stored for long periods of time and are harder to identify.

## SCRIPT FOR CHEMISTRY II CLASS FORENSIC CASE

### Part I: Announcing the Murder

- Come in during the first 15 minutes of each class and pull me [the teacher] out of class.
- When we go back into class, I can make the following announcement:
  - "I have some breaking news in the forensic case you all have been working on for the police department. Larry J. has been found dead with several bullet wounds to the chest."
  - If they ask any additional questions, we will just say this information is "classified at this time."

### Part II: Crime Scene Analysis

- Then you will discuss the tests that need to be done in this kind of a case. Discuss the following tests that the police department needs the students to complete:
  - Test #1: Fingerprinting (latent prints from the gun; what latent prints are and the process of dusting for them; if you have a dusting kit where you could show how prints are lifted off a coffee mug or something else that would be great.)
  - Test #2: Bullet Matching (from the gun to the bullet at the crime scene or matching bullets at the crime scene to other bullets at the crime scene)
  - Test #3: Gunshot Residue (we will be doing an acid–base titration for this but you can talk about how it is actually done)
  - Test #4: Blood (you can talk about DNA but our test will not involve that; it will probably involve a pH test or a reaction of the chemicals in the blood)
- For each of the tests explain why those tests are done and how they can match or not match suspects to the scene of the crime. You can discuss which tests are more conclusive than others and why.

### Part III: Lab Work

- I will have all the labs set up already for the tests they need to do, so after you are done speaking I will announce that we need to perform the tests you just spoke about. I will announce that "we will start work on this case right away."
- This does not need to take the whole hour…if you could just talk for about 10–15 minutes about the four different tests, that would work out great.

## FINGERPRINT EVIDENCE CHART

### ARREST CARD

Document Control Number | Ref. DCN

L31611125

Arresting agency ORI-NCIC

Transaction Control Number

FRM0130L31611125

Subject Last Name

First Name

Middle Name/Suffix

Photo Available — Yes

Palm Prints Available — Yes

Arrestee Armed With
(Choose maximum of two)

| | | | |
|---|---|---|---|
| Unarmed | ☐ | Unknown Firearm | ☐ |
| Handgun | ☐ | Rifle | ☐ |
| Shotgun | ☐ | Other Firearm | ☐ |
| Lethal Cutting Instrument | ☐ | | |
| Club/ Blackjack/ Knuckles | ☐ | | |

| Automatic Weapon | ☐ |
|---|---|

| Adjustment Term | | Term | y/m/d/hrs |
|---|---|---|---|
| Community Mediation | M | | |
| Community Service | X | | |
| Contact Limitations | L | | |
| Counseling | U | | |
| Curfew | C | | |
| Geographic Restrictions | G | | |
| Juvenile Officer Reporting | J | | |
| Peer Support Program | P | | |
| Possession of Firearms Limitations | F | | |
| Restitution | R | | |
| School Attendance Required | S | | |
| Other | O | | |
| Specify Length of Term by placing term followed by y/m/d/hrs | | | |

| Arrest Type | |
|---|---|
| On View Arrest | V |
| Summoned/Cited | S |
| (Not Taken into Custody) | |
| Original Arrest Warrant | A |
| Bond Forfeiture Warrant | B |
| Probation Violation Warrant | P |
| Probation/ Mandatory Supervised | |
| Release Violation Warrant | M |
| Out of State Warrant | O |

### Parent/ Legal Guardian (Please Print)

Name:_____

Address:_____

Employer:_____

Home Phone:_____ Work Phone:_____

Relationship:_____

**Please Send This Copy To:**
**Local Police Department**

### Finger Print Images

| 1. R. THUMB | 2. R. INDEX | 3. R. MIDDLE | 4. R. RING | 5. R. LITTLE |
|---|---|---|---|---|
| 6. L. THUMB | 7. L. INDEX | 8. L. MIDDLE | 9. L. RING | 10. L. LITTLE |

| LEFT FOUR FINGERS TAKEN SIMULTANEOUSLY | L. THUMB | R. THUMB | RIGHT FOUR FINGERS TAKEN SIMULTANEOUSLY |
|---|---|---|---|

Name:_____ Class:_____ Date:_____

# The Case of Kirsten K.:
# *The Weapon Analysis Evidence*

## PART I: THE FINGERPRINT ANALYSIS

### *Case Background*

Larry J. has been found murdered with several bullet wounds to the chest. Two guns were found at the crime scene: one next to the victim with the handle wrapped in aluminum foil, and the other, with a unique copper handle, at the bottom of a garbage can outside the cellar door to Gladys V.'s lake house. The police need your help to collect and analyze the fingerprints found on the aluminum foil and copper handle to determine if the prints match any of the suspects and/or victim. Samples from each gun handle are ready for analysis.

### *Background Information on Fingerprint Classification*

Latent prints cannot be seen by the naked eye and often have to be dusted in order to see the patterns more clearly. Every person has a unique set of fingerprints, but three basic patterns allow forensic scientists to classify them. The three basic patterns are the whorl, the arch, and the loop. **Whorl** patterns have lots of circles that do not leave either side of the print. **Arch** patterns have lines that start on one side of the print, rise toward the center, and leave on the other side of the print. **Loop** patterns have lines that start on one side of the print, rise toward the center, turn back, and leave on the same side from which they started. Fingerprints are permanent; they form during fetal

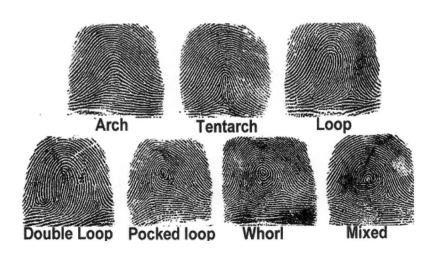

Arch    Tentarch    Loop

Double Loop    Pocked loop    Whorl    Mixed

development and start in the basal layer of the skin. Fingerprints always grow in the same place and any damage to the basal layer becomes permanent.

## Procedure

### Aluminum Foil Handle Fingerprints

1. Examine the print first on the aluminum sample before dusting to identify whose print it most closely matches based on the prints in the evidence envelope.
2. Dust the fingerprints with the powder and brushes provided. Be careful not to destroy the print when dusting with the brush.
3. After dusting the print with the brush, preserve the print by placing the clear tape over the dusted print on the aluminum foil.
4. Try to match the print to the suspect/victim prints in the evidence envelope.

### Copper Handle Fingerprints

1. Examine the print first on the copper sample before dusting to identify whose print it most closely matches based on the prints in the evidence envelope.
2. Dust the fingerprints with the powder and brushes provided. Be careful not to destroy the print when dusting with the brush.
3. After dusting the print with the brush, preserve the print by placing the clear tape over the dusted print, then lifting the tape and the print off of the copper metal sample.
4. Stick the tape with the print on it onto a piece of white paper to preserve the print.
5. Try to match the print to the suspect/victim prints in the evidence envelope.

## Materials

- Dusting powder and brushes
- Fingerprint samples
- Clear tape
- White paper

## Data

Construct a table to identify which types of fingerprints are on each of the gun handles and to whom the prints belong from the suspect list.

## Conclusion

1. Who are the possible matches to the aluminum foil fingerprints?

_____

_____

2. Who are the possible matches to the copper handle fingerprints?

_____

_____

3. Are there any suspects that can be ruled out at this point for the murders of Kirsten K. and her husband, Larry J.? Explain.

_____

_____

_____

# PART II: GUN AND BULLET MATCHING

## Background Information

Police have run the set of unknown fingerprints found on the gun handles through AFIS (Automatic Fingerprint Identification System) to try to match them to anyone in the system with a previous criminal record. After running these prints, a match for the unknown fingerprints has been found. Pick up a suspect list to find out more information about all the suspects, including the new suspect #5.

Bullets from each of the guns (aluminum and copper) were found at the scene of the crime as well. During the autopsy, remnants of silver bullets were found in the victim's chest. After a sweep of the crime scene, both silver and zinc bullets were found in the basement. The police need your help to match the bullets to the appropriate gun so they can start to piece together what happened the day of the murder.

The electric potential for each gun and bullet combination has to be within a certain range for the bullet to be compatible with the gun type. To match each gun metal and bullet metal type in the correct combination, they must have an electric potential difference between 0 and +1.0 V. In each case, the gun metal will be oxidized and the bullet metal will be reduced.

## Analysis: Calculations

Show all calculations below to prove which of the metal bullets belongs to each gun.

Write the overall redox reaction and the standard cell notation for each of the gun/bullet combinations.

## Conclusion

1. Which bullet type was matched to which gun and what evidence proves this?

   _____
   _____
   _____
   _____

2. Based on the evidence so far, which gun do you believe belonged to which suspect and which do you believe belonged to the victim, Larry J.?

   _____
   _____

# PART III: GUNSHOT RESIDUE

## Background Information

All suspects have been brought in for a final questioning, during which time they were swabbed for gunshot residue on their hands. The gunshot residue swab has been placed in a solution of HCl. Police need your help in analyzing the suspects and the victim, Larry J., to see if the solutions show any signs of gunshot residue. A positive match for gunshot residue will show an acid concentration of 0.15 M or higher.

## Procedure

1. Put 10ml of each of the solutions for each titration into a 250 ml Erlenmeyer flask.
2. Dilute the 10 ml of the solutions with 35 ml of distilled water, yielding a total solution of 45 ml to be titrated.
3. Add 2–3 drops of the phenolphthalein indicator to the flask.
4. Fill the buret with the NaOH (base) solution provided.
5. Record the initial and final volumes of the base in the buret to determine how much of the 0.1 M NaOH solution it took to titrate each sample.
6. Perform and record **at least** one trial for each of the solutions.

## Data

Create a data table similar to the one provided below to record the initial amount of acid used, initial reading of the buret, and final reading of the buret for each of the suspects and the victim, Larry J.

| | HAROLD M. | GLADYS V. | ELIZABETH G. | LARRY J. | GERALD V. |
|---|---|---|---|---|---|
| Amount of Acid from suspect sample | | | | | |
| Initial Buret Reading | | | | | |
| Final Buret Reading | | | | | |
| Volume of NaOH used | | | | | |

## Analysis: Calculations

Use the space below to show calculations for the acid concentration in each of the gunshot residue swabs from the solutions for each of the suspects and the victim.

Write the balanced neutralization reaction for the acidic solution with the basic solution.

1. Suspect #1: Harold M.

   _____

   _____

   _____

2. Suspect #2: Gladys V.

   _____

   _____

   _____

3. Suspect #3: Elizabeth G.

   _____

   _____

   _____

4. Suspect #4: New Victim: Larry J.

   _____

   _____

   _____

5. Suspect #5: Gerald V.

   _____

   _____

   _____

## Conclusion

1. Who had positive matches for the gunshot residue? Who had negative matches for gunshot residue? Explain your results.

   _____

   _____

2. How does this evidence help to narrow down the suspects? What are possible scenarios at this point for what happened in the basement of Gladys V.'s lake house?

   _____

   _____

# PART IV: BLOOD STAIN ANALYSIS

## Background Information

Clothes from each of the suspects and victim have been taken to determine if the stains found on the clothes are blood stains. Your job is to determine which clothing items contain blood and identify the stains that are not blood.

## Data: Part A

Each of the blood stains must fall within a pH range of 6.5-8.0 to be considered actual human blood. For each of the following pieces of data, calculate the pH from the information given. If the stain believed to be blood is too small, only the [OH-] concentration could be obtained. If the sample believed to be blood is large enough, the [$H_3O^+$] concentration could be obtained.

## TABLE 1

PH RANGE CALCULATIONS TO DETERMINE BLOOD STAINS

| SUSPECT INFORMATION | [$H_3O^+$] (CONCENTRATIONS LISTED FOR # OF STAINS FOUND) | [OH-] | PH | BLOOD STAIN: YES OR NO? |
|---|---|---|---|---|
| Victim: Kirsten K. | (1) $1.00 \times 10^{-7}$ M | — | | |
| Suspect #1: Harold M. | — | (1) $3.16 \times 10^{-4}$ M | | |
| Suspect #2: Gladys V. | — | (1) $3.16 \times 10^{-7}$ M | | |
| Suspect #3: Elizabeth G. | — | (1) $1.00 \times 10^{-10}$ M | | |
| Suspect #4: New Victim: Larry J. | (1) $3.16 \times 10^{-7}$ M (2) $3.16 \times 10^{-8}$ M | — | | |
| Suspect #5: Gerald V. | — | (1) $3.16 \times 10^{-7}$ M (2) $1.00 \times 10^{-7}$ M (3) $3.16 \times 10^{-8}$ M | | |

## Analysis: Calculations Part A

Show your calculations to fill in Table 1.

## Data: Part B

Further tests have been done on the stains that were proven to fall into the pH range matching the pH of blood from 6.5–8.0. More than one stain may have been found on more than one piece of clothing. Tests were done to see if the pH values that were calculated in Table 1 match any of the blood types from each of the suspects who were found to have blood on them.

### TABLE 2

**BLOOD TYPES AND PH LEVELS**

| BLOOD TYPE | PH LEVEL |
|---|---|
| A | 8.0 |
| B | 7.0 |
| AB | 7.5 |
| O | 6.5 |

### TABLE 3

**BLOOD TYPES OF SUSPECTS AND VICTIMS**

| SUSPECT INFORMATION | BLOOD TYPE |
|---|---|
| Victim: Kirsten K. | B |
| Suspect #2: Gladys V. | A |
| Suspect #4: New Victim: Larry J. | O |
| Suspect #5: Gerald V. | AB |

## Analysis: Calculations Part B

Calculate the pH of each of the samples from Table 4 to see which ones match the blood types provided in Table 2 and Table 3.

### Conclusion

1. Which of the suspects and/or victims had stains that fell into the pH range of blood? (from Table 1)

2. Why may Harold M. have shown a basic stain and Elizabeth G. have shown an acidic stain? You may have to look back at previous assessments and/or suspect files.

3. After further calculations for those suspects with blood stains, which of the suspects/victims did those stains prove to be a match to? (from Table 4)

4. What are possible scenarios to link both of the murders of Kirsten K. and Larry J.? Is there more than one suspect who could be responsible for the murder? Does the evidence lead one way or another?

### TABLE 4:

**BLOOD PH MATCHING**

| SUSPECT INFORMATION | $[H_3O+]$ OF BLOOD SAMPLE 1 | $[H_3O+]$ OF BLOOD SAMPLE 2 | $[H_3O+]$ OF BLOOD SAMPLE 3 | SUSPECT/VICTIM MATCHES |
|---|---|---|---|---|
| Kirsten K. | $1.00 \times 10^{-7}$ M | — | — | |
| Larry J. | $3.16 \times 10^{-7}$ M | $3.16 \times 10^{-8}$ M | — | |
| Gerald V. | $3.16 \times 10^{-7}$ M | $1.00 \times 10^{-7}$ M | $3.16 \times 10^{-8}$ M | |
| Gladys V. | $3.16 \times 10^{-8}$ M | — | — | |

# SUSPECT FILE D

**Victim: Kirsten K.**

- No new information

**Suspect #1: Harold M.**

- Started his own plumbing business
- Is a licensed gun owner

**Suspect #2: Gladys V.**

- Just received the Hunters Unlimited Alumni Volunteer Award
- Has a deer permit issued for the current hunting season

**Suspect #3: Elizabeth G.**

- Eloped in Las Vegas with her longtime boyfriend
- Made her own wedding cake for the occasion

**Suspect #4: Larry J.—NEW VICTIM**

- Body found in the basement of Gladys V.'s lake house

**Suspect #5: Gerald V.**

- Son of Gladys V.
- Has a deer permit issued for the current hunting season
- Lives with Gladys V. in the lake house

Name:_____ Class:_____ Date:_____

# Student Lab Report Example:
## *The Weapon Analysis Evidence*

## I. INTRODUCTION

### (A) Background Information

From the previous investigation on the Kirsten K. case, the police have recently discovered that Larry J. (Kirsten's widowed husband), has been found murdered. His body was found with several bullet wounds in the chest. The police have also discovered that there were two guns used at the crime scene. The gun found by the victim's body had aluminum foil wrapped around the handle. While the second gun with a unique copper handle was found just outside of Gladys V.'s cellar door at the bottom of a garbage can. The police then realized that they would need the help of forensic scientists to analyze the two guns for fingerprints to possibly help identify the murderer of Larry J., and make any connections to the case of Kirsten K. The police used the AFIS (automatic fingerprint identification system) to try to link the unknown fingerprints found on the gun to any new suspects. After the fingerprints were run through the system they were identified as a new suspect's set of prints, Gerald V., son of Gladys V. During the autopsy for Larry J., there were remnants of silver bullets found in the victim's chest; and while doing a sweep through of the crime scene there were both silver and zinc bullets found in the basement. During all of the suspects' last questioning, they were swabbed for gunshot remnants on their hands. Those were then placed into a solution of HCl and the police had to wait for the results. While the ballistics of gun matching to the bullets will be important, it will be more important to see which suspects test positive for gunshot residue. Also there were clothes that were taken from the suspects and victim to see whether or not there were any found blood stains. Finding which suspects have blood stains on them and who the blood stains belong to will help provide convicting evidence police can use to solve both murders of Kirsten K. and Larry J.

### (B) Purpose

The purpose is to determine the most likely suspects based on the new evidence collected from the fingerprints, gunshot residue, and blood analysis.

## II. DATA

### Part I: The Fingerprint Evidence

## TABLE 1

**FINGERPRINT MATCH**

| Handle Type | Type of Fingerprint | Person's Identity |
|---|---|---|
| Copper Fingerprint 1 | Whirl | Gladys V. |
| Copper Fingerprint 2 | Loop | Unknown Print #1 |
| Aluminum Fingerprint 1 | Tentarch | Larry J. |
| Aluminum Fingerprint 2 | Pocketed Loop | Unknown Print #1 |

### Part III: Gunshot Residue

## TABLE 2

**GUNSHOT RESIDUE TEST**

| | Harold M. | Gladys V. | Elizabeth G. | Larry J. | Gerald V. |
|---|---|---|---|---|---|
| Amount of Acid from suspect sample (ml) | 10 ml | 10 mL | 10 ml | 10 ml | 10 ml |
| Initial Buret Reading (ml) | 0.00 ml | 0.00 ml | 0.00 ml | 0.20 ml | 0.00 ml |
| Final Buret Reading (ml) | 12 ml | 13 ml | 10.5 ml | 42.3 ml | 44.6 ml |
| Volume of NaOH (ml) | 12 ml | 13 ml | 10.5 ml | 42.1 ml | 44.6 ml |
| Positive or Negative for Gunshot Residue | Negative | Negative | Negative | Positive | Positive |

## Part IV: Blood Stain Analysis
## TABLE 3

**BLOOD ANALYSIS**

| Suspect Info | $[H_3O+]$ | $[OH-]$ | pH | Blood Stain (Yes or No) | Blood Match |
|---|---|---|---|---|---|
| Victim: Kirsten K. | $1.0 \times 10^{-7}$ | | 7 | Yes | Her own blood |
| #1: Harold M. | | $3.16 \times 10^{-4}$ | 10.5 | No | Basic stain from plumbing job |
| #2: Gladys V. | | $3.16 \times 10^{-7}$ | 7.5 | Yes | Gerald V. |
| #3: Elizabeth G. | | $1 \times 10^{-10}$ | 4 | No | Acidic stain (glyoxylic acid) from making of vanilla from cake shop |
| #4: New Victim: Larry J. | $3.16 \times 10^{-7}$  $3.16 \times 10^{-8}$ | | 6.5  7.5 | Yes  Yes | Larry J.  Gerald V. |
| #5: Gerald V. | | | 7.5  7  6.5 | Yes  Yes  Yes | His own blood  Kirsten K.  Larry J. |

# III. ANALYSIS: CALCULATIONS

## Part II: Gun and Bullet Matching

| Type of Reaction | Half Reaction Combinations | Reaction Potentials (V) | Cell Potential (V) |
|---|---|---|---|
| LEO | Al → Al$^{+3}$ +3e- | 1.66 | = 0.9 V* |
| GER | Zn$^{+2}$ + 2e- → Zn | -0.76 | |
| LEO | Al → Al$^{+3}$ +3e- | 1.66 | = 2.46 V |
| GER | Ag$^{+1}$ + 1e- → Ag | 0.80 | |
| LEO | Cu → Cu$^{+2}$ + 2e- | -0.34 | = -1.10 V |
| GER | Zn$^{+2}$ + 2e- → Zn | -0.76 | |
| LEO | Cu → Cu$^{+2}$ + 2e- | -0.34 | = 0.46 V* |
| GER | Ag$^{+1}$ + 1e- → Ag | 0.80 | |
| *=fits within the range of 0 Volts to +1.0 Volts, to show a bullet to gun match, so the aluminum gun goes with the zinc bullets and the copper gun goes with the silver bullets | | | |

## Part III: Gunshot Residue

## Calculations for the Gunshot Solutions' Concentrations

Step 1: Balance the Neutralization Reaction

$$1HCL + 1NaOH \rightarrow 1NaCl + 1H_2O$$

Step 2: Use the equation molarity = moles/L to find the moles of base

| Harold M. | Gladys V. | Elizabeth G. | Larry J. | Gerald V. |
|---|---|---|---|---|
| = moles/0.012 | = moles/0.013 | 0.1 = moles/0.0105 | 0.1 = moles/0.0421 | 0.1 = moles/0.0446 |
| = 0.0012 moles | = 0.0013 moles | = 0.00105 moles | = 0.00421 moles | =0.00446 moles |

Step 3: Find the moles of acid by using mole to mole calculations

| Harold M. | 0.0012 moles × $\dfrac{1 \text{ mole HCl}}{1 \text{ mole NaOH}}$ = 0.0012 moles HCl |
|---|---|
| Gladys V. | 0.0013 moles × $\dfrac{1 \text{ mole HCl}}{1 \text{ mole NaOH}}$ = 0.0013 moles HCl |
| Elizabeth G. | 0.00105 moles × $\dfrac{1 \text{ mole HCl}}{1 \text{ mole NaOH}}$ = 0.00105 moles HCl |
| Larry J. | 0.00421 moles × $\dfrac{1 \text{ mole HCl}}{1 \text{ mole NaOH}}$ = 0.00421 moles HCl |
| Gerald V. | 0.00446 moles × $\dfrac{1 \text{ mole HCl}}{1 \text{ mole NaOH}}$ = 0.00446 moles HCl |

Step 4: Find the molarity of the acid using the molarity equation

| Harold M. | Gladys V. | Elizatbeth G. | Larry J. | Gerald V. |
|---|---|---|---|---|
| M = 0.0012/0.01 | M = 0.0013/0.01 | M = 0.00105/0.01 | M = 0.00421/0.01 | M = 0.00446/0.01 |
| = 0.12 M | =0.13 M | =0.105 M | =0.421 M | =0.446 M |

## Part IV: Blood Stain Analysis
### PH CALCULATIONS

| Suspect Info | $[H_3O^+]$ M | $[OH^-]$ M | pH | Calculations |
|---|---|---|---|---|
| Victim: Kirsten K. | $1.0 \times 10^{-7}$ | | 7 | $pH = -\log [H_3O^+]$<br>$pH = -\log [1.0 \times 10^{-7}]$<br>$pH = 7$ |
| #1: Harold M. | | $3.16 \times 10^{-4}$ | 10.5 | $pOH = -\log [OH^-]$<br>$pOH = -\log [3.16 \times 10^{-4}]$<br>$pOH = 3.5$<br>$pOH + pH = 14$<br>$+ pH = 14$<br>$pH = 10.5$ |
| #2: Gladys V. | | $3.16 \times 10^{-7}$ | 7.5 | $pOH = -\log [OH^-]$<br>$pOH = -\log [3.16 \times 10^{-7}]$<br>$pOH = 6.5$<br>$pOH + pH = 14$<br>$6.5 + pH = 14$<br>$pH = 7.5$ |
| #3: Elizabeth G. | | $1 \times 10^{-10}$ | 4 | $pOH = -\log [OH^-]$<br>$pOH = -\log [1 \times 10^{-10}]$<br>$pOH = 10$<br>$pOH + pH = 14$<br>$+ pH = 14$<br>$pH = 4$ |
| #4: New Victim: Larry J. | (a) $3.16 \times 10^{-7}$<br><br>(b) $3.16 \times 10^{-8}$ | | (a) 6.5<br><br>(b) 7.5 | (a) $pH = -\log [H_3O^+]$<br>$pH = -\log [3.16 \times 10^{-7}]$<br>$pH = 6.5$<br>(b) $pH = -\log [H_3O^+]$<br>$pH = -\log [3.16 \times 10^{-7}]$<br>$pH = 7.5$ |
| #5: Gerald V. | | (a) $3.16 \times 10^{-7}$<br><br><br><br>(b) $1.00 \times 10^{-7}$<br><br><br><br>(c) $3.16 \times 10^{-8}$ | (a) 7.5<br><br><br><br>(b) 7<br><br><br><br>(c) 6.5 | (a) $pOH = -\log [OH^-]$<br>$pOH = -\log [3.16 \times 10^{-7}]$; $pOH = 6.5$<br>$pOH + pH = 14$<br>$6.5 + pH = 14$<br>$pH = 7.5$<br>(b) $pOH = -\log [OH^-]$<br>$pOH = -\log [1 \times 10^{-7}]$; $pOH = 7$<br>$pOH + pH = 14$<br>$7 + pH = 14$<br>$pH = 7$<br>(c) $pOH = -\log [OH^-]$<br>$pOH = -\log [3.16 \times 10^{-8}]$; $pOH = 7.5$<br>$pOH + pH = 14$<br>$7.5 + pH = 14$<br>$pH = 6.5$ |

# IV. CONCLUSION

## *Part I: The Fingerprint Analysis*

Who are the possible matches to the aluminum foil fingerprints? Who are the possible matches to the copper handle fingerprints? Are there any suspects that can be ruled out at this point for the murders of Kirsten K. and her husband Larry J.? Explain.

The possible match for the aluminum foil fingerprint can/may belong to Larry J., the new victim and husband of Kirsten K. There is also an unknown fingerprint that was found on the aluminum gun handle. As for the copper gun, there is a print that matches Gladys V.'s prints, who is an avid hunter as she was recently issued a deer permit. And the same unknown print that was on the aluminum gun handle was also on the copper gun handle. So the only suspect thus far that can be completed ruled out for the murder of Larry J. is Elizabeth G., although she is still a prime suspect in the murder of Kirsten K. Elizabeth G. has also recently eloped with her longtime boyfriend, which means there may not have been an affair with Larry after all. Gerald V. will still be under surveillance because of his deer license as well, and the fact that he might have some valuable information on the case, which it comes to his mother. Harold M. can most likely be ruled out as being a suspect in both murders. There is little evidence that leads to him being at the crime scene since his fingerprints were not on the guns, he did not have gunshot residue on his hands, and the stains that were on him were not blood.

## *Part II: Gun and Bullet Matching*

Which bullet type was matched to which gun and what evidence proves this? Based on the evidence you have so far, which gun do you believe belonged to which suspect and which do you believe belonged to the victim, Larry J.?

The bullet and gun that were matched together from the calculations above were the aluminum gun with the zinc bullet and the copper gun with the silver bullet. This makes sense that Larry's prints would have been on the aluminum gun since that was most likely the gun that belonged to Larry. The silver bullets that were in Larry's chest most likely came from Gerald's gun, because it is not probable that Larry would have shot himself in the chest. So from this discovery I believe that the gun that had the zinc bullet belonged to the new victim, Larry J. While the aluminum gun with the silver bullet belonged to the suspect, Gerald V.

## *Part III: Gunshot Residue*

Who had positive matches for the gunshot residue? Who had negative matches for gunshot residue? Explain your results. How does this evidence help to narrow down the suspects? What are possible scenarios at this point for what happened in the basement of Gladys V.'s lake house?

The positive matches for the gunshot residue were the new victim Larry J., with an acid concentration of 0.421M and Gerald V. who had an acid concentration of 0.446M. So all of the other suspects were negative for the gunshot residue, and this consisted of Harold M. (0.012M), Gladys V. (0.13M), and Elizabeth G. (0.105M). So just from this test, the police can narrow the murder of Larry J. to just one suspect, which is the son of Gladys V., the one whom none of the police or forensic scientist ever knew about until now. A possible scenario would be that Larry J. owed Gladys V. and Gerald V. money for his drug habit so they took his wife, Kirsten K. for ransom. When Larry J. could not pay the ransom because he didn't have the money, he had to meet with Elizabeth G. to see if she could loan him some money from her business. Larry J. cut off Kirsten K.'s ring finger to get her wedding ring off after he found her dead body in the woods around the lake. Because Larry J. was angry about Gerald V. killing his wife, he went over to the lake house to confront him, which turned into his murder.

## Part IV: Blood Stain Analysis

Which of the suspects and/or victims had stains that fell into the pH range of blood? (from Table 1) Why may have Harold shown a basic stain and Elizabeth have shown an acidic stain? You may have to lookback at previous assessments and/or suspect files. After further calculations for those suspects with blood stains, which of the suspects/victims did those stains prove to be a match to? (from Table 4) What are possible scenarios to link both of the murders of Kirsten K. and Larry J.? Is there more than one suspect who could be responsible for the murder? Does the evidence lead one way or another?

Just from looking at blood analysis data, it states that the new victim Larry J., the original victim Kirsten K., Gladys V., and Gerald V. all had a pH between the ranges of 6.5–8.0, which tells the police that there was a blood stain on their piece of clothing. Now the reasons why Harold M.'s result showed a basic stain was because he works with plumbing while for Elizabeth G. she works around cakes and pastries all day. So after further calculations for those suspects, it shows that there are matches between Gerald V., and both Larry J. and the original victim Kirsten K. From reading all the results, I think that the murderer of both Larry J. and Kirsten K. is Gerald V. A possible scenario is that Gerald V. had an obsession for Kirsten K., he knew that she was married, and that she was unhappy in her relationship but would not leave her husband, because of fear... so Gerald V. killed her in anger. Then Gerald V. killed Larry J., since he was the reason Kirsten K. was not free to be with him.

# GRADING RUBRIC D

Name _____

Score _____ /40 _____ % _____ Grade ____

## I. Introduction

| Application | # | wgt | Exemplary (10) | At Standard (8) | In Progress (7) | Still Emerging (6) | No Evaluation (0) |
|---|---|---|---|---|---|---|---|
| Defining Problems | 1a | * | Definition of problem or issue reflects a broad, insightful view (4 of 4)<br>☐ **Background Information** for Part I is summarized by saying what will be proven with each test<br>☐ **Background Information** for Part II is summarized by saying what will be proven with each test<br>☐ **Background Information** for Part III is summarized by saying what will be proven with each test<br>☐ **Background Information** for Part IV is summarized by saying what will be proven with each test | Definition of problem or issue is reasonable and concise (3 of 4) | Definition of problem has aspects that are vague or incomplete (2 of 4) | Overall definition of problem is vague or unreasonable (1 of 4) | No work shown for this section |

## II. Data

| Application | # | wgt | Exemplary (10) | At Standard (8) | In Progress (7) | Still Emerging (6) | No Evaluation (0) |
|---|---|---|---|---|---|---|---|
| Interpreting Models | 1b | * | Interprets visuals or models at a complex level (4 of 4)<br>☐ Data table for Part I: Fingerprint Analysis includes a table of what fingerprints are matches to which suspects<br>☐ Data table for Part III: Gunshot Residue shows all titration data from each suspect's titration<br>☐ Data table for Part IV: Blood Stain Analysis—two tables are reconstructed from Table 1 and Table 4 data to show blood stain and suspect matches<br>☐ Correct **titles and units** are used for all data tables required for this assessment | Interprets visuals or models at a general level (3 of 4) | Interpretation of visuals or models contains errors that restrict understanding (2 of 4) | Shows fundamental errors in use and understanding of visuals (1 of 4) | No work turned in for this section |

## III. Analysis: No Graph Needed
## III. Analysis: Calculations

| Application | # | wgt | Exemplary (10) | At Standard (8) | In Progress (7) | Still Emerging (6) | No Evaluation (0) |
|---|---|---|---|---|---|---|---|
| Problem Calculations | 2a | * | All essential information is evident through well-organized work while justifying the solution (4 of 4)<br>☐ Electrochemistry calculations for **Part II: Gun and Bullet Matching** for matching the bullet to the gun are complete, correct, and ALL WORK is included along with units for all numbers throughout calculation<br>☐ The overall redox reaction and the standard cell notation are shown for each gun/bullet combination for **Part II: Gun and Bullet Matching** | Most essential information is evident through organized work while leading to the solution (3 of 4) | Minimum information is evident through work with a solution present (2 of 4) | Work is extremely unorganized with no solution present (1 of 4) | No work shown for this section |

| | | | Exemplary (10) | At Standard (8) | In Progress (7) | Still Emerging (6) | No Evaluation (0) |
|---|---|---|---|---|---|---|---|
| | | | ☐ Calculations and the balanced neutralization reaction for **Part III: Gunshot Residue** for the titration of each suspect sample are complete and correct<br>☐ Calculations for **Part IV: Blood Analysis** for the Table 1: Blood stain data are complete, correct, and ALL WORK is included along with units for all numbers throughout the calculation | | | | No work shown for this section |

## IV. Conclusions

| Application | # | wgt | Exemplary (10) | At Standard (8) | In Progress (7) | Still Emerging (6) | No Evaluation (0) |
|---|---|---|---|---|---|---|---|
| Connecting Ideas | 1d | * | Makes insightful connections between ideas or events that might not be obvious—abstract thinking evident (4 of 4)<br>☐ **Part I conclusion:** All questions are answered and suspect/data collection information from Part I is considered in the answers<br>☐ **Part II conclusion:** All questions are answered and suspect/data collection information from Part II is considered in the answers<br>☐ **Part III conclusion:** All questions are answered and suspect/data collection information from Part III is considered in the answers<br>☐ **Part IV conclusion:** All questions are answered and suspect/data collection information from Part IV is considered in the answers | Makes general, logical connections between ideas or events; mostly concrete in nature (3 of 4) | Makes superficial connections between ideas; thinking might be confused or incomplete (2 of 4) | Makes incorrect or no connections between ideas (1 of 4) | |

## Overall Report Formatting (Extra Credit—5 points)

| Application | # | wgt | |
|---|---|---|---|
| Technology Applications | 1c | * | Technology used is best available and appropriate for the required research, data representation, interpretation, and communication of results.<br>☐ Entire Lab Report is computer generated (5 points); including data tables and calculations typed using the computer |

## CHAPTER 7 — *The Drug Lab Evidence*

## CHEMISTRY CONTENT

- IR Spectra
- Organic Functional Groups
- Thin Layer Chromatography
- $R_f$ Values
- Solvents and Solutions

## NATIONAL SCIENCE EDUCATION STANDARDS ADDRESSED

Content Standard A: Science as Inquiry
Content Standard B: Physical Science
Content Standard G: History and Nature of Science

## CASE INFORMATION

Police have learned some additional information about the suspects involved in this case, and their relationship to the victim. These details are provided in the Suspect File and have been summarized as follows: Suspect #1, Harold M., just purchased a lake house on Clinton Lake, the scene of the crime. Gladys V., suspect #2, is a retired pharmacist but still stays in contact with past customers. The year before she retired, Gladys V. was suspended by her employer for the possible illegal activity involving the misuse of pharmaceuticals. Suspect #3, Elizabeth G, has a business at normal productivity. Gerald V., Suspect #5, recently planned a fishing trip to Canada for the third year in a row.

After the police investigation of the crime scene where Larry J.'s body was found, a drug lab was discovered in the basement of the V. residence, containing multiple baby food jars of some sort of unknown drug. Police have found an unknown drug in the basement and need you to do some further testing on the drug to determine what was being made and sold out of the basement. This will help police determine the connection of Larry J. to the V.'s and also provide insight into Kirsten's murder as well. This is the final assessment, so it is important to gather as much evidence as possible so that students can put all the evidence together in a plausible scenario for the murders and the connections of all the suspects.

### Part I: The IR Spectra Analysis

Police have mixed up the infared spectroscopy (IR Spectra) for each of the chemicals found in the basement in the baby food jars. Students are expected to look at the given IR Spectra and match the spectra to the three chemicals: acetaminophen, caffeine, and aspirin. Students use their knowledge of functional groups and IR Spectra to match each of the mixed up spectra to the appropriate chemical. Chemical structures, as seen in Figure 7.1, are given to the students so they can see what functional groups they are looking for when they look at the peaks of the spectra. This part of the assessment does not give students any evidence toward the case, but it does assess their knowledge of functional groups and reading IR Spectra charts.

## FIGURE 7.1

**CHEMICAL STRUCTURES OF THREE SUBSTANCES: ASPIRIN, CAFFEINE, AND ACETAMINOPHEN**

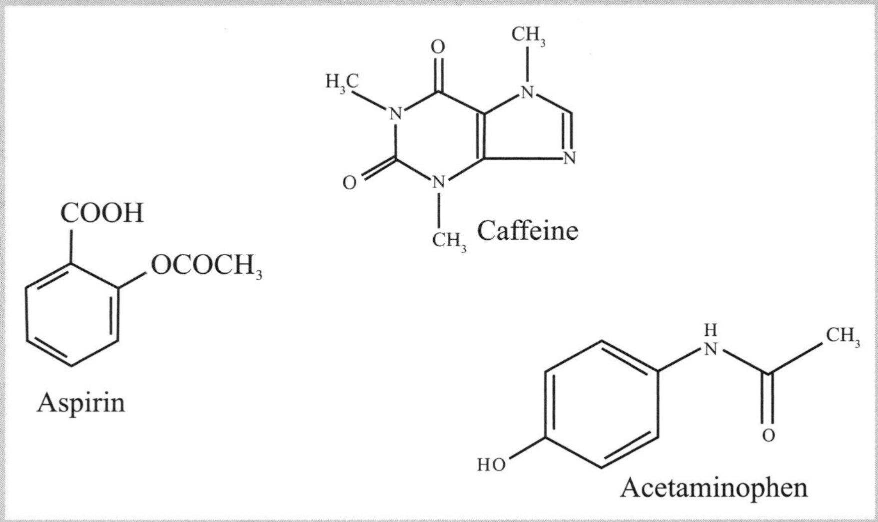

## Part II: Caffeine Extraction

A plastic storage container of coffee grounds was found in the basement of the lake house, and police think that Gerald V. was extracting caffeine from the coffee to make the unknown drug. In Part II of this assessment, the students determine if caffeine can be extracted from coffee and if so, how much could be extracted from the amount the police found in the basement. Students will need to figure out how much caffeine can be extracted from the amount of coffee grounds found in Gladys V. and Gerald V.'s basement.

Students generally have no problem following the procedure for the extraction of caffeine. The only part students run into problems with is that they have to decant the top layer of solution containing the caffeine from the rest of the coffee solution. Students will often use a pipet to suction the layer of solution away from the rest of the coffee solution.

You can tell if students are successful or not because the decanted solution will be an orange color and not the brown color of coffee.

> I usually make the coffee solution using 50 g of instant coffee in 1,000 ml of water. You can choose the amount of coffee and water you want to use to make the solution, but you have to tell the students the amounts of coffee and water used so they can set up a proportion for how much caffeine they extract from that amount of coffee.

### Part III: Thin Layer Chromatography of an Unknown Drug

Students look at the chromatography papers for each of the known chemicals: acetaminophen, aspirin, and caffeine. I used to have the students make their own thin layer chromatography papers for each chemical for each group. Thin layer chromatography (TLC) paper is expensive, so to save money, I saved the papers that I made when making the solutions and taped them to manila folders. Then I marked where the solution started and ended for each chemical, and also where the solvent started and ended, so that students could calculate the $R_f$ values for each of the known chemicals to compare those to the $R_f$ values of the chemicals in the unknown drug, as seen in Figure 7.2.

Students will find that the two chemicals in the unknown drug are caffeine and aspirin. When we were making this assessment, we did not have a particular known drug in mind with that combination. However, as luck would have it, I had a student in my class whose father was a pharmacist, and he informed us that prescription migraine medicine often contains both caffeine and aspirin. While this may not seem highly illegal, it would still be illegal to manufacture drugs in the basement that are not approved, but yet safe enough that this scenario can be used in a school setting.

If you want students to perform the TLC process themselves, Flinn Scientific, Inc., has a kit containing vials of each of the chemicals used in this assessment. The TLC paper just has to be repurchased each year and the solutions of each chemical need to be made fresh each year before this assessment.

### Part IV: Thin Layer Chromatography of Pen Matching

Police found a drug log book in the basement that they think was used for recording drug transactions. Police have confiscated pens from Gladys V., Larry J., and Gerald V. to test to see if they match the pen

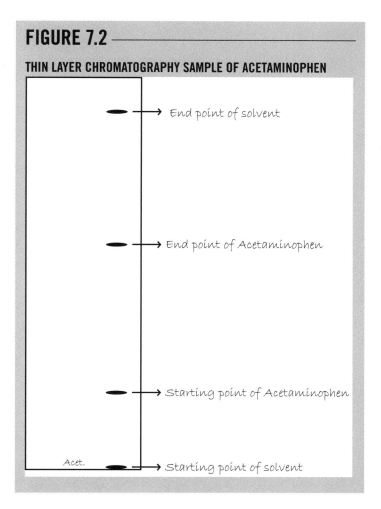

**FIGURE 7.2**

**THIN LAYER CHROMATOGRAPHY SAMPLE OF ACETAMINOPHEN**

End point of solvent

End point of Acetaminophen

Starting point of Acetaminophen

Acet.

Starting point of solvent

ink in the drug log book and to see if there was a drug connection between any of the victims and suspects. Students use filter paper cut into strips and make a pen marking on it from each of the pens provided in the baggies and labeled with forensic tags. Students place the filter papers into a beaker with fingernail polish remover (acetone) in it as the solvent. As the solvent moves up the paper, various colors appear on the filter paper, producing different streaks for each type of ink. You need to make sure you have pens that will make different chromatograms and then make sure they are in the correctly labeled bags for each suspect (and stay that way throughout student testing of the pens). I also make a police evidence folder that has chromatograms that are already made so students can match their evidence to that in the folder to conclude which suspects' pens were being used to write in the drug log book. The ink pens should match Larry J. and Gladys V., thereby connecting Larry J. to the possibility of illegal drug distribution and providing motive for a murder in the drug basement at Gladys V.'s house.

In the remaining pages of this chapter, you will find a teacher guide, student handout, suspect file, student lab report example, and grading rubric for Performance Assessment 5: The Drug Lab Evidence. More information about how to use the grading rubric for this and future performance assessments can be found in Appendix B.

# Teacher Guide:
## *The Drug Lab Evidence*

**Time:** 4–5 days
**Grades:** 11 and 12 (second-year chemistry)

## OBJECTIVES

1. Students will solve a forensics case using their knowledge of chemistry (for performance assessment #5, this includes naming compounds, organic functional group naming and identification, infrared spectroscopy, and thin layer chromatography).
2. Students will assemble their evidence and present their case at the end of the year.
3. Students will answer four questions:

### Part I

1. Can any of the compounds be matched with unknowns from previous evidence?

### Part II

1. How much total caffeine could be extracted from the coffee found in the basement?

### Part III

1. Which substances were found in the unknown drug?

### Part IV

1. Which suspect pen(s) match the ink on file from the drug logbook?

## PREPARATION

### Part I

You will need to make an evidence folder for each student group with the three unlabeled IR spectra. Students will create a data table to show which peaks from the IR spectra match which frequencies based on their knowledge of the organic compound and its various functional groups. You will also need to provide students with a chart of typical IR Spectra absorption frequencies. The IR Spectra and frequency charts are provided at the end of this teacher guide.

### Part II

Dissolve 50 g of instant caffeinated coffee in 1,000 ml of distilled water. You may have to heat the water to get all of the coffee to dissolve. Each group will use 100 ml of this coffee solution for the lab.

### Part III

For this activity, the unknown solution will contain caffeine and aspirin. One possible explanation for this combination would be a migraine medicine.

### Part IV

You must use *three* different pens of the same color to produce three different TLC chromatographs (e.g., felt tip, marker, and ballpoint pen). Put each pen in a labeled baggie with a forensic tag detailing where each pen was found and from which suspect it came. You will also need to make evidence samples to which students can match their TLC samples in order to determine which suspect pens match the ink found in the drug log. Since students rotate from station to station for this lab assessment, you will only need one evidence folder with the evidence ink samples in it.

## QUESTION GUIDELINES

For calculations, formulas, and work, see the student example at the end of the chapter.

### Part I

1. The unknown #2 on Larry J. from Performance Assessment #2: The Chemical Evidence can be identified as caffeine.

### Part II

1. Yes, they should be able to extract caffeine crystals.
2. Depends on the amount the students are able to extract from the coffee solution
3. Discolored if not properly decanted.

### Part III

1. Caffeine and aspirin were present in the unknown drug.

### Part IV

1. The pens of Larry J. and Gladys V. match the ink samples from the logbook.

## MATERIALS

In addition to the materials listed within the student assessment handout, the following materials will also be needed:

- Suspect File E
- Student Assessment Handout
- IR Spectra of caffeine, aspirin, and acetaminophen (included at the end of the teacher guide)
- TLC materials (Flinn Scientific, Inc. FB1648: Identification of Unknown Substances II)
- Ink evidence folder from the drug logbook (2)
- Suspect pens (3)

## TEACHER HINTS

### Part III

While you may want to include some evidence of a suspect or victim having migraines, this may not be the only drug that Gerald was making in the drug lab, so we wanted to keep it general for the students to be able to create their final scenarios.

### Possible Scenario

Gladys and her son were using the basement of the lake house to synthesize their own drugs. Her son, Gerald V., would make the drugs, and then Gladys V. would sell them to her customers on the side. When Gladys V. rented the lake house to the victim, Kirsten K., she did not inform her son. The victim walked into the lake house, only to find a surprised Gerald V. working away in the basement. After she discovered what he was doing, she threatened to inform the police. Gerald V. killed the victim. Afraid of going to jail, he called his mother. Gladys V. helped her son dispose of the body and much of the evidence; however, they couldn't get rid of everything. Larry J., while snooping around the lake house trying to find any clues as to his wife's death, came across the drug lab in the lake house basement. He was then killed (could also be a drug deal gone bad since Larry J.'s name was found in the book). The police were then called to the scene where they found the final pieces of evidence.

## TABLE 7.1

### TABLE OF INFRARED ABSORBANCES FOR COMMON ORGANIC FUNCTIONAL GROUPS

| Table of Infrared Absorbances for Common Organic Functional Groups | |
|---|---|
| Functional Group | Characteristic Absorption(s) in $cm^{-1}$ |
| Alkane C-H Stretch | 2950-2850 (m or s) |
| Alkene C-H Stretch | 3100-3010 (m) |
| Alkene C=C Stretch | 1680-1620 (v) |
| Alkyne C-H Stretch | ~3300 (s) |
| Alkyne C≡C Stretch | 2260-2100 (v) |
| Aromatic C-H Stretch | ~3030 (v) |
| Aromatic C-H Bending | 860-680 (s) |
| Aromatic C=C Bending | 1700-1500 (m) |
| Alcohol O-H Stretch | 3550-3200 (broad, s) |
| Carboxylic Acid O-H Stretch | 3000-2500 (broad, v) |
| Carboxylic Acid C=O Stretch | 1780-1710 (s) |
| Amine N-H Stretch | 3500-3300 (m) |
| Aldehyde C=O Stretch | 1740 –1690 (s) |
| Ketone C=O Stretch | 1750-1735 (s) |
| Ester C=O Stretch | 1750-1735 (s) |
| Amide C=O Stretch | 1690-1630 (s) |
| Amide N-H Stretch | 3700-3500 (m) |
| Ether C-O Stretch | 1200-1070 |

In the table above, signal intensity (peak height) is denoted by the following abbreviations: w = weak, m = medium, s = strong, and v = variable.

# TABLE 7.2

**INFRARED ABSORPTION FREQUENCIES CHART**

Infrared Absorption Frequencies Chart

| Functional Class | Characteristic Absorptions |
|---|---|
| **Sulfur Functions** | |
| **S-H** thiols | 2550–2600 cm$^{-1}$ (wk & shp) |
| **S-OR** esters | 700–900 (str) |
| **S-S** disulfide | 500–540 (wk) |
| **C=S** thiocarbonyl | 1050–1200 (str) |
| **S=O** sulfoxide | 1030–1060 (str) |
| sulfone | 1325± 25 (as) & 1140± 20 (s) (both str) |
| sulfonic acid | 1345 (str) |
| sulfonyl chloride | 1365± 5 (as) & 1180± 10 (s) (both str) |
| sulfate | 1350–1450 (str) |
| **Phosphorous Functions** | |
| **P-H** phosphine | 2280–2440 cm$^{-1}$ (med & shp) |
| | 950–1250 (wk) P-H bending |
| **(O=)PO-H** phosphonic acid | 2550–2700 (med) |
| **P-OR** esters | 900–1050 (str) |
| **P=O** phosphine oxide | 1100–1200 (str) |
| phosphonate | 1230–1260 (str) |
| phosphate | 1100–1200 (str) |
| phosphoramide | 1200–1275 (str) |
| **Silicon Functions** | |
| **Si-H** silane | 2100–2360 cm$^{-1}$ (str) |
| **Si-OR** | 1000–11000 (str & brd) |
| **Si-CH$_3$** | 1250± 10 (str & shp) |
| **Oxidized Nitrogen Functions** | |
| **=NOH** oxime | |
| O-H (stretch) | 3550–3600 cm$^{-1}$ (str) |
| C=N | 1665± 15 |
| N-O | 945± 15 |
| **N-O** amine oxide | |
| aliphatic | 960± 20 |
| aromatic | 1250± 50 |
| **N=O** nitroso | 1550± 50 (str) |
| nitro | 1530± 20 (as) & 1350± 30 (s) |

**INFRARED ABSORPTION FREQUENCIES CHART (continued)**

| Functional Class | Stretching Vibrations | | | Bending Vibrations | | |
|---|---|---|---|---|---|---|
| | Range ($cm^{-1}$) | Intensity | Assignment | Range ($cm^{-1}$) | Intensity | Assignment |
| Alkanes | 2850–3000 | str | $CH_3$, $CH_2$, & CH 2 or 3 bands | 1350–1470 / 1370–1390 / 720–725 | med / med / wk | $CH_2$ & $CH_3$ deformation / $CH_3$ deformation / $CH_2$ rocking |
| Alkenes | 3020–3100 / 1630–1680 / 1900–2000 | med / var / str | =C-H & $=CH_2$ (usually sharp) / C=C (symmetry reduces intensity) / C=C asymmetric stretch | 880–995 / 780–850 / 675–730 | str / med / med | =C-H & $=CH_2$ (out-of-plane bending) / cis-RCH=CHR |
| Alkynes | 3300 / 2100–2250 | str / var | C-H (usually sharp) / C≡C (symmetry reduces intensity) | 600–700 | str | C-H deformation |
| Arenes | 3030 / 1600 & 1500 | var / med-wk | C-H (may be several bands) / C=C (in ring) (2 bands) (3 if conjugated) | 690–900 | str-med | C-H bending & ring puckering |
| Alcohols & Phenols | 3580–3650 / 3200–3550 / 970–1250 | var / str / str | O-H (free), usually sharp / O-H (H-bonded), usually broad / C-O | 1330–1430 / 650–770 | med / var-wk | O-H bending (in-plane) / O-H bend (out-of-plane) |
| Amines | 3400–3500 (dil. soln.) / 3300–3400 (dil. soln.) / 1000–1250 | wk / wk / med | N-H (1°-amines), 2 bands / N-H (2°-amines) / C-N | 1550–1650 / 660–900 | med-str / var | $NH_2$ scissoring (1°-amines) / $NH_2$ & N-H wagging (shifts on H-bonding) |
| Aldehydes & Ketones | 2690–2840(2 bands) / 1720–1740 / 1710–1720 / 1690 / 1675 / 1745 / 1780 | med / str / str / str / str / str / str | C-H (aldehyde C-H) / C=O (saturated aldehyde) / C=O (saturated ketone) / aryl ketone / α, β-unsaturation / cyclopentanone / cyclobutanone | 1350–1360 / 1400–1450 / 1100 | str / str / med | α-$CH_3$ bending / α-$CH_2$ bending / C-C-C bending |
| Carboxylic Acids & Derivatives | 2500–3300 (acids) overlap C-H / 1705–1720 (acids) / 1210–1320 (acids) / 1785–1815 ( acyl halides) / 1750 & 1820 (anhydrides) / 1040–1100 / 1735–1750 (esters) 1000–1300 / 1630–1695(amides) | str / str / med / str / str / str / str / str | O-H (very broad) / C=O (H-bonded) / O-C (sometimes 2-peaks) / C=O / C=O (2-bands) / O-C / C=O / O-C (2-bands) / C=O (amide I band) | 1395–1440 / 1590–1650 / 1500–1560 | med / med / med | C-O-H bending / N-H (1°-amide) II band / N-H (2°-amide) II band |
| Nitriles | 2240–2260 | med | C≡N (sharp) | | | |
| Isocyanates, Isothiocyanates, Diimides, Azides, Ketenes | 2100–2270 | med | -N=C=O, -N=C=S / -N=C=N-, -N₃, C=C=O | | | |

**IR SPECTRA OF CHEMICAL SUBSTANCES**

Unknown A is

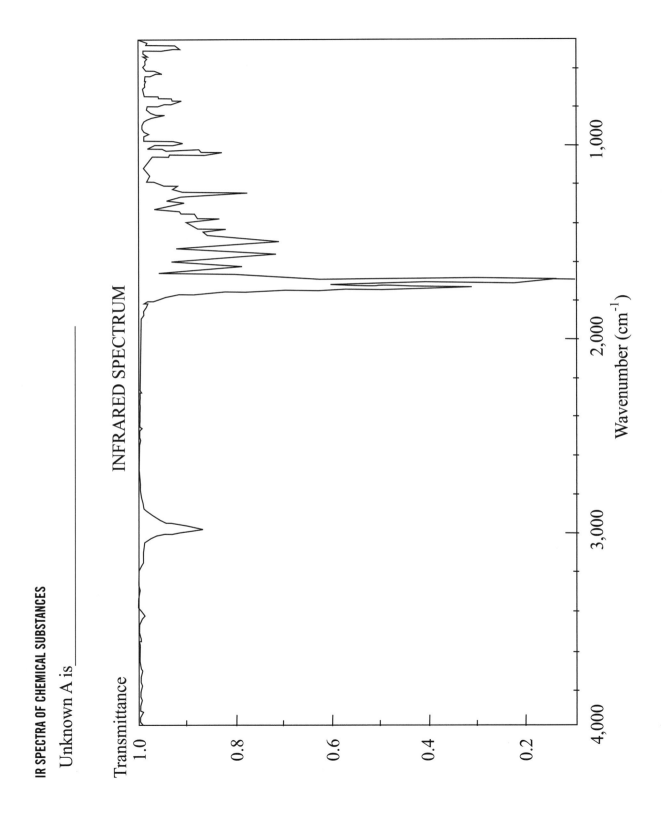

INFRARED SPECTRUM

**IR SPECTRA OF CHEMICAL SUBSTANCES (CONTINUED)**

Unknown B is _____

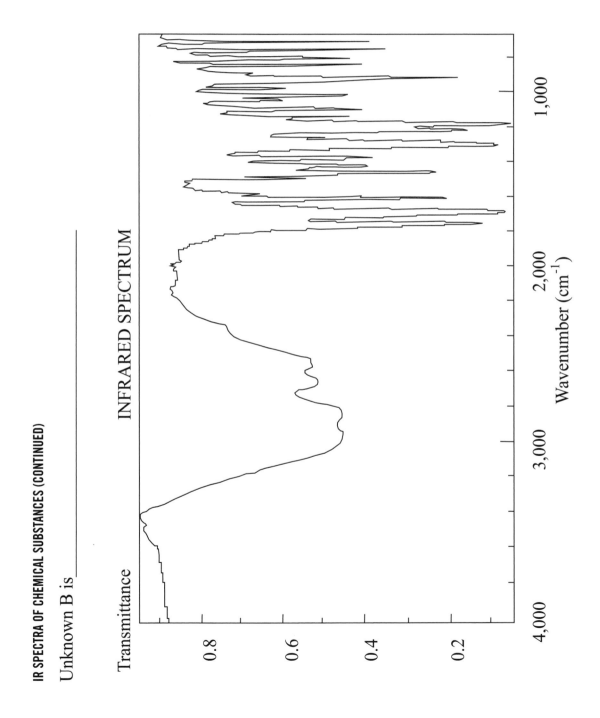

INFRARED SPECTRUM

**IR SPECTRA OF CHEMICAL SUBSTANCES (CONTINUED)**

Unknown C is _____

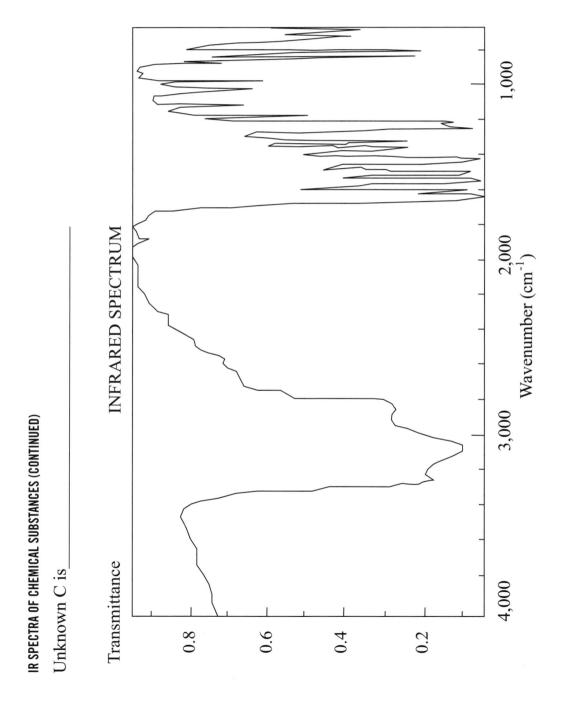

INFRARED SPECTRUM

Name:_____Class:_____Date:_____

# The Case of Kirsten K.:
## *The Drug Lab Evidence*

## PART I: THE IR SPECTRA ANALYSIS

### *Case Background*

After further investigation, police have uncovered what they think to be a drug lab in the basement of the lake house where the murder of Larry J. took place. Reports indicate that Gerald V. was frequently seen entering the cellar door that leads to the drug lab. Police uncovered the following:

- 3 "substances" in baby food jars labeled aspirin, caffeine, and acetaminophen
- A large plastic container filled with 2,240 g of coffee grounds
- Multiple bottles of what appears to be some sort of unknown drug

The police suspect the aspirin, caffeine, and acetaminophen were being used to create this unknown drug, and that someone was extracting the caffeine from coffee. Additionally, the police found a small spiral-bound notebook with a list of names, dates, and transactions. The police have determined that this list consists of people who bought the drugs made in this lab. One of the names on the list was Larry J.. Finally, Gerald V.'s fingerprints were found on the baby food jars and on the bottles of unknown drugs.

The CSI unit of the local police department is requesting your help in order to solve this crime once and for all. It is up to you to assemble these final pieces of evidence, determine who should be charged with the murders of Kirsten K. and her husband, Larry J., and also present if there are any additional charges the killer(s) could be facing. Good Luck! (Be sure to tie up any loose ends still remaining from other parts of the investigation).

In order to acquire detailed chemical information about the substances found in the baby jars, police investigators took the samples to the forensics lab, where they ran some IR spectra analysis. Unfortunately, the officer carrying the file of the spectra dropped the folder, and the IR spectra got mixed up. You need to determine which IR spectrum belongs to each of the three substances in the baby food jars.

### *Materials*

- IR Spectra of three substances (acetaminophen, aspirin, caffeine)

### *Data*

1. Research has been completed about the three substances (aspirin, caffeine, and acetaminophen). What are their empirical formulas?

|  | Molecular formula | Empirical formula |
|---|---|---|
| Aspirin: | $C_9H_8O_4$ | _____ |
| Caffeine: | $C_8H_{10}N_4O_2$ | _____ |
| Acetaminophen: | $C_8H_9NO_2$ | _____ |

2. Clearly circle and identify all organic functional groups present in each of the molecules.

Aspirin          Caffeine          Acetaminophen

3. Use the research you have collected to determine which IR spectrum from the evidence envelopes belongs to each of the substances. Create a data table below that shows which peaks for each spectra correspond to which functional groups and wavelengths.

# PART II: CAFFEINE EXTRACTION

## Background Information

Police want to know if caffeine can actually be extracted from the coffee grounds, and if so, how much total caffeine could be extracted from all of the coffee grounds found in the plastic container in the basement of the lake house.

## Purpose

To determine if caffeine can be extracted from coffee grounds

## Procedure

1. To a clean 500 ml Erlenmeyer flask, add 100 ml of coffee extract. This extract is the solution that was prepared in advance by the instructor.

2. Add approximately 2 g of sodium bicarbonate to the coffee solution. This will react with some of the substances in the coffee extract and make them extremely water soluble. Swirl the mixture until all the sodium carbonate dissolves.

3. Add 25 ml of ethyl acetate and vigorously swirl the mixture for 10 minutes. Do not shake the mixture.

4. Allow the mixture to stand and separate into two layers, a dark aqueous bottom layer and a clear ethyl acetate top layer.

5. Carefully pour off as much of the clear layer as possible into a beaker, being careful not to remove the bottom layer. This process is called decanting.

6. Place a 12.5 cm fluted filter paper in a long stem glass funnel. Put the funnel in a small iron ring and suspend it over a 250 ml Erlenmeyer flask.

7. Using a squeeze bottle of water, thoroughly wet the filter paper.

8. Slowly and carefully pour the ethyl acetate/water mixture into the fluted filter paper. The excess water will drain through and the ethyl acetate solution of caffeine will remain on the filter paper.

9. Using a pipette, transfer the ethyl acetate solution to a 50 ml Erlenmeyer flask. To this solution, add a scoop of anhydrous sodium sulfate in order to remove the last traces of water.

10. While the solution is drying, weigh a 50 ml beaker to the nearest 0.01 g. Record this in the data table. Tare the scale.

11. Using a pipette, transfer the dried solution to the 50 ml beaker.

12. Evaporate most of the ethyl acetate in the hood on a warm hot plate. When only a fraction of a milliliter of liquid is left, remove the beaker from the hot plate. Allow the beaker to stand in the hood for a minute or two. The heat remaining in the glass will cause the last amount of ethyl acetate to evaporate and produce a solid residue of crude caffeine.

13. In order to determine your recovery of caffeine, reweigh the cool beaker and record this mass in the data table.

## Materials

- Coffee solution
- 500 ml Erlenmeyer flask
- 250 ml beaker
- Filter paper
- Iron ring
- Solid sodium bicarbonate
- Balance
- Pipette
- Hot plate
- Methylene chloride/ethyl acetate
- Funnel
- Anhydrous sodium sulfate
- 50 ml beaker

## Data

***Instructor Notes: Coffee extract solution prepared with 50 g of coffee/1,000 ml

### CAFFEINE EXTRACTION DATA

| | |
|---|---|
| **Mass of Empty 50ml beaker** | |
| **Mass of 50ml beaker and Caffeine** | |
| **Mass of Caffeine** | |

## Conclusion/Discussion Questions

1. Were you able to obtain caffeine crystals from the coffee ground solution?

2. How much total caffeine could be extracted from all of the coffee grounds found in the basement?

3. Describe the appearance of your product. Caffeine is a white solid, but your product was probably discolored. Why?

## PART III: THIN LAYER CHROMATOGRAPHY OF AN UNKNOWN DRUG

### Background Information

Thin layer chromatography (TLC) is one technique that is commonly used to identify unknown drugs. You will use TLC to identify the components contained in the bottles of unknown drug found at the scene. You will use the three substances (aspirin, caffeine, and acetaminophen) as your known solutions to determine if any of them are also apparent in the unknown drug.

### Purpose

To determine the components in the unknown drug

### Procedure

1. Cut appropriate size chromatography paper (if not already cut for you). Handle the paper by the edges.
2. Mark a pencil line across the bottom of the chromatography paper and label a spot for each solution tested.

3. Apply 6–8 drops of each solution onto the TLC paper (3 known and 1 unknown), using capillary tubes, to the labeled spots on the pencil line.

4. Add solvent (ethyl acetate) to the beaker/bottle. Make sure the line with the solution spots will not be submerged in the solvent.

5. Run the solvent at least 6–7 cm up the paper.

6. Mark a solvent front (or the height to which the solvent went) with a pencil.

7. Measure the distance the solvent moved and the distance each component of the solutions moved.

8. Calculate the $R_f$ values for each of the solutions in the Analysis section.

## Materials

- Development jar with lid
- TLC plate, 4 in. × 2 in.
- Aspirin standard solution, 6–10 drops
- Acetaminophen standard solution, 6–10 drops
- Caffeine standard solution, 6–10 drops
- "Unknown" solution
- UV light source
- Ethyl acetate
- Microcapillary tubes, 4
- Ruler
- Pencil

## Data

Design a data table that shows the distance traveled for the compound and the solvent, as well as $R_f$ values for each of the known substances and the unknown drug.

## Analysis: Calculations

Use the space below to show $R_f$ value calculations based on the equation given below.

$$R_f \text{ value} = \frac{\text{distance traveled by compound}}{\text{distance traveled by solvent}}$$

## Conclusion

What component(s) were present in the unknown drug?

# PART IV: THIN LAYER CHROMATOGRAPHY OF PEN MATCHING

## Background Information

The police have acquired pens from each of the suspects and the new victim, Larry J.. They have run an ink analysis on the information found in the spiral notebook. You will perform a chromatography test on each of the pens to see if any of them match the ink from the drug log book where Larry J.'s name was found recorded several times.

## Purpose

To determine whose pen can be matched to the ink from the drug log.

## Procedure

1. Cut the filter paper into three strips. Label with a pencil at the top of each piece of filter paper, which suspect the pen belongs to.
2. Make a horizontal mark (about 1 in. from the bottom) with one of the pens across one of the pieces of filter paper. Repeat this with each pen and each piece of filter paper.
3. Pour the solvent into the bottom of each of the beakers so that the solvent does not reach the mark made by the pen.
4. Get the evidence folder and try to match the evidence filter papers with those from the pens from each of the suspects.

## Materials

- Suspect pens (Gladys V., Gerald V., Larry J.)
- Ink from drug log
- Coffee filters or filter paper
- Fingernail polish remover (acetone)

## Data

Construct a data table to record any qualitative and/or quantitative observations about each of the suspect samples compared to the evidence samples.

## Conclusion

1. Which pen(s) match the ink samples from the drug log book?

2. What can you conclude, if anything, from the new information presented in relation to the crime?

## THE FINAL SCENARIO

Record the final scenario, linking all of the assessments together and evidence to support all theories in the case. Who should be convicted and for what crimes?

*Kirsten K. Murder Case*

*Larry J. Murder Case*

# SUSPECT FILE E

### Victim: Kirsten K.

- No new information

### Suspect #1: Harold M.

- Just bought his own house on the lake

### Suspect #2: Gladys V.

- Is a retired pharmacist but still stays in contact with past customers
- In her last year of work in 2001 she was suspended for possible illegal activity involving the misuse of pharmaceuticals from her employer

### Suspect #3: Elizabeth G.

- Her cake business is back to its normal productivity level prior to disappearance of Kirsten K.

### Suspect #4: Larry J.—NEW VICTIM

- No new information

### Suspect #5: Gerald V.

- Recently planned a fishing trip to Canada for the third year in a row

Name:_____ Class:_____ Date:_____

# Student Lab Report Example:
## *The Drug Lab Evidence*

## I. INTRODUCTION

### *(A) Background Information*

Police have begun their investigation in the basement of Gladys V.'s lake house where Larry J. was found murdered with bullet wounds to the chest. Police have discovered there are 3 substances labeled aspirin, caffeine, and acetaminophen that are stored in baby food jars. There is also a large plastic container with 2,240 g of coffee grounds. Also, there are several bottles of what appears to be an unknown drug. Police think the three chemicals (aspirin, caffeine, and acetaminophen) are somehow being used to create the new unknown drug and that caffeine was being extracted from the coffee grounds. Police have run IR spectra for each of the three substances but have mixed them up and you need to match the IR spectra to the correct substance. Police need to also test to see if caffeine can in fact be extracted from coffee, and if so, how much can be extracted from the amount found in Gladys V.'s basement. A thin layer chromatography test was run on the unknown drug and the three known substances to see if there are any matches to the unknown drug, so that police can start to piece together what is being made illegally in the basement of the lake house. Lastly, there was what looked like a drug log book where all the drug transactions have been recorded. Pens from the remaining suspects need to be analyzed to see if their Thin layer chromatograms match the ink from the drug log book.

### *(B) Purpose*

The purpose is to match the IR Spectra of the three known substances and to determine the most likely suspects based on the new evidence collected from the caffeine extraction lab, and thin layer chromatography from the unknown drug and the suspect pens.

## II. DATA

### Part I: IR Spectra Analysis

| IR Spectra | Substance Match | Molecular Formula | Empirical Formula | Functional Groups | Wavenumber (cm⁻¹) |
|---|---|---|---|---|---|
| A | Caffeine | $C_8H_{10}N_4O_2$ | $C_4H_5N_2O$ Matches Unknown #1 found on Larry J. in PA#2 | Amide (N-C=O) Amine (N-C) C=O | 3000 (weak) 1630–1695 (strong) |
| B | Aspirin | $C_9H_8O_4$ | $C_9H_8O_4$ | Aromatic (C=C and C-H) Carboxylic acid (O-H; C=O) Ester (C=O) | 1200–1600 (several peaks) 800 (several peaks) 3200–3550 (medium; broad) 1800 (strong) 1750 (strong) |
| C | acetaminophen | $C_8H_9NO_2$ | $C_8H_9NO_2$ | Aromatic (C=C) Alcohol (O-H) Amide (N-C=O) | 1200–1600 (several peaks) 3200–3550 (strong; broad) strong |

### Part II: Caffeine Extraction

**CAFFEINE EXTRACTION DATA**

| Measurements | Mass (grams) |
|---|---|
| Mass of Empty 50 ml Beaker | 30.943 g |
| Mass of 50 ml Beaker and Caffeine | 31.043 g |
| Mass of Caffeine | 0.100 g |

### Part III: Thin Layer Chromatography of an Unknown Drug

| Substance | Distance Solvent Traveled (centimeters) | Distance Substance Traveled (centimeters) |
|---|---|---|
| Caffeine | 4.21 cm | 3.76 cm |
| Aspirin | 3.23 cm | 1.98 cm |
| Acetaminophen | 2.80 cm | 1.25 cm |
| Unknown (1 and 2) | (1) 3.84 cm (2) 3.84 cm | (1) 2.37 cm (2) 3.50 cm |

## Part IV: Thin Layer Chromatography of Pen Matching

| Suspect's Pen | Pen Chromatography Description | Match to Ink in Log Book (Yes or No) |
|---|---|---|
| Gladys V.' purse | Top left = purple<br>Bottom = yellow | Yes |
| Larry J.'s hand | Top left = dark purple | Yes |
| Gerald V.'s pocket | Top = blue/gray | No |

# III. ANALYSIS: CALCULATIONS

## Part II: Caffeine Extraction

Step 1 → Amount of coffee in student sample

$$\frac{50\ g\ coffee}{1{,}000\ mL\ water} = \frac{x}{100\ ml\ water}$$

$$x = 5\ g\ coffee\ in\ student\ sample$$

Step 2 → Ratio of caffeine in coffee to amount in tub

$$\frac{0.1\ g\ of\ caffeine}{5\ g\ of\ coffee} = \frac{x}{2240\ g\ of\ coffee}$$

$$x = 44.8\ g\ of\ caffeine$$

## Part III: Thin Layer Chromatography of an Unknown Drug

| Substance | $R_f$ value calculations |
|---|---|
| Caffeine | $R_f = \dfrac{3.76}{4.21} = 0.893$ |
| Aspirin | $R_f = \dfrac{1.98}{3.23} = 0.613$ |
| Acetaminophen | $R_f = \dfrac{1.25}{2.80} = 0.446$ |
| Unknown | Substance 1 → <br> $R_f = \dfrac{2.37}{3.84} = 0.617$ <br><br> Substance 2 → <br> $R_f = \dfrac{3.50}{3.84} = 0.911$ |

# IV. CONCLUSION

## *Part I: The IR Spectra Analysis*

Can any of the compounds be matched with unknowns from previous evidence?

The mixed up IR Spectra have been matched with the correct substance. IR Spectra A was found to be caffeine because it is the only substance that does not have the O-H bond that shows a very strong, broad peak around a wavenumber of 3,000. IR Spectra B was found to be aspirin because of the weaker O-H peak shown at a wavenumber of 3,000 when compared to the O-H peak in IR Spectra C. The alcohol functional group found in the acetaminophen shows a much stronger peak at a wavenumber of 3,000 than the O-H group in aspirin that is part of a carboxylic acid functional group. The empirical formula for caffeine matches the empirical formula for the Unknown #1 from the performance assessment #2: chemical evidence. The unknown #2 was found on Larry and at the crime scene. This would show a connection of Larry J. to Gerald V. and Gladys V. and the drug lab in the basement of the lake house long before he was murdered. Also, the caffeine could have gotten to the crime scene from Gerald V., since Gerald V. also had the blood of the first victim, Kirsten K., on him, from evidence in Performance Assessment #4. The evidence at this time would lead to Gerald V. as being the prime suspect in the murders of Kirsten K. and Larry J.

## *Part II: Caffeine Extraction*

How much total caffeine could be extracted from the coffee found in the basement?

Caffeine can be extracted from coffee according to the lab procedure conducted in this part of the evidence collection. This means that caffeine was most likely being extracted from the coffee grounds to create a new more powerful drug in the basement of the lake house. Further testing will need to be done to determine exactly how the caffeine from the coffee was being used. The total amount of caffeine that could be extracted from the 2,240 g of coffee found in the basement in the plastic container was calculated to be 44.8 grams. The caffeine looked more brown that white, but that is most likely because it was stained from being in the coffee and then being extracted using the lab procedure and chemicals involved.

## *Part III: Thin Layer Chromatography of an Unknown Drug*

Which substances were found in the unknown drug?

According to the thin layer chromatography and the $R_f$ value calculations, the unknown drug contains aspirin and caffeine. The $R_f$ values for the unknown were found to be 0.617 and 0.911, which are the closest to the values of caffeine (0.893) and aspirin (0.613). The only logical explanation for the combination of these two drugs is that Gerald V. and Gladys V. were creating a strong migraine medicine. While this may not seem highly illegal, it is still illegal to manufacture and sell any type of medicine that is not approved by the FDA (Food and Drug Administration).

## Part IV:

Which suspect pen(s) match the ink on file from the drug log book?

The pens found on Larry J. and Gladys V. match the drug log book ink. The pen found on Larry J. could indicate that he was involved somehow in the drug business that Gladys V. and Gerald V. were running out of their basement. The pen could have also been planted on Larry J. after his death by Gerald V. or Gladys V. to make Larry J. look more involved in the business than he was. Larry J.'s name was found in the drug log book for some recent transactions, which proves that he was at least purchasing the drugs that were being made in the basement. Both Gladys V. and Gerald V. have drug convictions in their past. Gerald V. had drug possession charges and intent to sell on his record, and Gladys V. was suspended by her employer for the misuse of pharmaceuticals while she was working at the pharmacy. Gerald V. has a fishing trip planned to Canada so police may want to have him stay in town until the investigation is finalized.

# GRADING RUBRIC E

Name _____

Score _____ /40     % _____     Grade _____

## I. Introduction

| Application | # | wgt | Exemplary (10) | At Standard (8) | In Progress (7) | Still Emerging (6) | No Evaluation (0) |
|---|---|---|---|---|---|---|---|
| Defining Problems | 1a | * | Definition of problem or issue reflects a broad, insightful view (4 of 4)<br>☐ **Background Information** for Part I is summarized by saying what will be proven with each test<br>☐ **Background Information** for Part II is summarized by saying what will be proven with each test<br>☐ **Background Information** for Part III is summarized by saying what will be proven with each test<br>☐ **Background Information** for Part IV is summarized by saying what will be proven with each test | Definition of problem or issue is reasonable and concise (3 of 4) | Definition of problem has aspects that are vague or incomplete (2 of 4) | Overall definition of problem is vague or unreasonable (1 of 4) | No work shown for this section |

## II. Data

| Application | # | wgt | Exemplary (10) | At Standard (8) | In Progress (7) | Still Emerging (6) | No Evaluation (0) |
|---|---|---|---|---|---|---|---|
| Interpreting Models | 1b | * | Interprets visuals or models at a complex level (4 of 4)<br>☐ Data table for Part I: A data table with title and units was created to show which peaks were used to identify each of the 3 substances<br>☐ Data table for Part II: Caffeine Extraction Lab data with units is included to show the amount of caffeine able to be extracted from the coffee<br>☐ Data table for Part III: Distances traveled by each substance and the $R_f$ values are shown for the known and the unknown drug; data table has title and units<br>☐ Data table for Part IV: Qualitative data from the pen chromatography is in a data table with a title | Interprets visuals or models at a general level (3 of 4) | Interpretation of visuals or models contains errors that restrict understanding (2 of 4) | Shows fundamental errors in use and understanding of visuals (1 of 4) | No work turned in for this section |

## III. Analysis: No Graph Needed
## III. Analysis: Calculations

| Application | # | wgt | Exemplary (10) | At Standard (8) | In Progress (7) | Still Emerging (6) | No Evaluation (0) |
|---|---|---|---|---|---|---|---|
| Problem Calculations | 2a | * | All essential information is evident through well-organized work while justifying the solution (4 of 4)<br>☐ Part II: the calculations for the amount of caffeine in the student sample of 100 ml of coffee are correct<br>☐ Part II: the calculations for the amount of caffeine that can be extracted from the 2,240 g of coffee in the container are correct<br>☐ Part III: $R_f$ value calculations are shown for the 3 substances TLC tested in the Drug Chromatography Lab<br>☐ Part III: $R_f$ value calculations are shown for the unknown TLC tested in the Drug Chromatography Lab | Most essential information is evident through organized work while leading to the solution (3 of 4) | Minimum information is evident through work with a solution present (2 of 4) | Work is extremely unorganized with no solution present (1 of 4) | No work shown for this section |

## IV. Conclusions

| Application | # | wgt | Exemplary (10) | At Standard (8) | In Progress (7) | Still Emerging (6) | No Evaluation (0) |
|---|---|---|---|---|---|---|---|
| Connecting Ideas | 1d | * | Makes insightful connections between ideas or events that might not be obvious—abstract thinking evident (4 of 4)<br><br>☐ **Part I conclusion:** ALL of the substances from the IR spectra are matched correctly and the correct substance is linked back to the correct unknown from PA #2: The Chemical Evidence<br><br>☐ **Part II conclusion:** All questions are answered and suspect/data collection information from Part II is considered in the answers to show the amount of caffeine that can be extracted<br><br>☐ **Part III conclusion:** All questions are answered and suspect/data collection information from Part III is considered in the answers for which substances are in the unknown drug<br><br>☐ **Part IV conclusion:** All questions are answered and suspect/data collection information from Part IV is considered in the answers to show which pens on the suspects match the ink in the drug log book | Makes general, logical connections between ideas or events; mostly concrete in nature (3 of 4) | Makes superficial connections between ideas; thinking might be confused or incomplete (2 of 4) | Makes incorrect or no connections between ideas (1 of 4) | No work shown for this section |

# CHAPTER 8
# *The Final Assessment*

## EVOLUTION OF THE FINAL PROJECT

As with all large projects, there are often many ways to approach the final assessment. Since the inception of this project, we have tried numerous methods to evaluate this yearlong performance assessment—some that worked, and some that did not. In the paragraphs that follow, we have outlined the successes and failures we have seen with this project as a whole. We realize that many other assessment methods exist, and we look forward to exploring those options as we continue to offer this curriculum in the future.

### What Worked: Design-Your-Own Project

Just as the individual performance assessments have evolved over the last years to make them clearer and easier to set up and evaluate, the final project has done the same. Last year, students chose the way they wanted to present their evidence from the case, based on some specific options provided for them:

- Create a concept map of the connections between the suspects and victims.
- Make a timeline of the evidence from start to finish.

- Assemble all of the evidence on a forensics board.
- Make a shadow box of the evidence from the crime scene.

Examples of each of these types of projects can be found at the end of this chapter. Students were also encouraged to develop their own projects if they thought of another way to compile their evidence collected throughout the year.

One advantage to this format of the final project assessment is that the students have a lot of flexibility in how they present the evidence from their case. In addition, they have the option to work in small groups or individually to complete the assessment. The variation in projects prevents the students (and the teacher) from becoming bored with the presentations. This method also allowed for flexibility in student schedules since many junior and senior level students miss time in class toward the end of the year for Advanced Placement exams. The disadvantage to this format is that it requires a little more effort on the teacher's part in order to properly assess the variety of projects. In addition, the first year this "design-your-own" project method was implemented, there were no student samples to show them. This year, however, we could show the students good and bad examples from the previous year, and we had developed a grading rubric, provided at the end of the chapter, to guide students through the expectations for putting all the evidence together. In the end, the "design-your-own" project method was the most successful and is still the method used today.

### What Didn't Work: PowerPoint Mania and Court Case Chaos

The first year we implemented this yearlong performance assessment in the classroom, we were developing the assessments as we progressed through each unit, not knowing where the students were going to end up with their final scenarios. To ensure that the students kept track of all the information throughout the year, they were required to keep a PowerPoint portfolio of all of the evidence they gathered from each assessment. Then at the end of the final assessment, each student presented their PowerPoint to the class in the auditorium as if they were presenting in a court case as the forensics scientist. Figure 8.1 shows a sample PowerPoint slide from one of the student presentations.

The advantage to this method of the final project assessment was that it allowed students the opportunity to compile their work throughout the year, requiring less work at the end of the year when they are often busy with many projects and tests from all of their courses. An advantage for the teacher was that the PowerPoints were easy to assess because each presentation had a specific, and uniform, checklist of requirements. However, this method did have its disadvantages—mainly that it was difficult for students, and the teacher, to sit through so many PowerPoint presentations, which all presented the same case with only minor changes in the final scenario. The process became monotonous for the audience, and as a result, this method was not used the following year.

After the PowerPoint overload, we knew we needed to alter the final assessment project, so we divided each class into two teams of students. Because

**FIGURE 8.1**

**STUDENT POWER POINT EXAMPLE OF THE FINAL SCENARIO**

**FINAL SCENARIO**

- Gladys stole substances from the pharmacy she worked at for Gerald to use in making drugs.

- Larry bought drugs from Gerald.

- Gerald had a secret admiration for Kirsten.

- This caused tension between Larry and Gerald.

- Gladys was willing to do anything for her son, giving her motive to kill Kirsten.

CRIME SCENE DO NOT CROSS    CRIME SCENE DO NOT CROSS

this curriculum was designed for a second-year chemistry course, there were both junior and senior level students, so it was easy to form the teams based on their grade level. Each group wrote a play script of a court case scenario based on all the evidence from each of the assessments. Figure 8.2 highlights a sample from one of the student scripts. The requirements specified that each person had to have a part in the court case and had to "be in character," which often meant costumes for each of the performers.

One advantage to this method of the final project assessment was that the students enjoyed watching the court cases. In addition, we incorporated other faculty at the school as the judge or jury for the case, so the students and teachers enjoyed that aspect as well. This method was superior to the PowerPoint method in that only two groups existed (juniors and seniors); therefore, there was not as much repetition of the case and the audience did not become bored. However, the major disadvantage to this method was that it was extremely hard to assess each individual on their knowledge of the evidence that they had been collecting all school year. Each student was to write their own part of the play, but typically only one or two students in each group of 10–12 were really in charge of writing the script and then everyone else was "hanging out" until it was time to practice reading through the script. In the end, this method was also discontinued. In the third year, the "Design-Your-Own" Project method was implemented and has been used ever since.

## FLEXIBILITY OF THE CASE

One of the major benefits to this curriculum is that the case is threaded throughout the entire school year of chemistry. In order for that method to be efficient, it requires that the case be flexible enough to follow the typical ebb and flow of a high school classroom in a typical school year. This means allowing not only flexibility for unanticipated delays such as school assemblies and snow days, but it also means allowing for the case itself to be flexible year to year so that the curriculum is reusable. This case can easily be altered so that the end result leads to a different suspect. The easiest way to alter the case would be to change the suspect number (for example, Elizabeth G. might become suspect #1 instead of suspect #3).

In addition to the entire case being flexible, the individual performance assessments are also relatively flexible, in that a few minor alterations can transform these performance assessments into stand-alone activities. We firmly believe in the power of this yearlong curriculum; therefore, we do not recommend dividing up the performance assessments as individual activities. However, we do recognize the restraints placed on teachers, and so we hope that all science teachers will be able to find something useful from the case of Kirsten K.

### FIGURE 8.2

#### STUDENT EXAMPLE OF A COURT CASE SCRIPT FOR THE MURDER OF KIRSTEN K.

**Bailiff-** All rise, Judge Brad presides over the case of Kirsten Knight-Jensen. (All rise)

**Judge-** You may be seated (all sit)

**Opening Arguments**

**Defense-** IT WAS LARRY! (Jury and audience mumble)

**Judge-** Order in the court! (bang gavel)

**Defense-** I am not here to dispute the fact that Elizabeth was at the scene, her shoe prints prove that. I'm here to prove that Larry was the killer. He had the closest amount of nitrate in the soil on his shoes as the nitrate in the soil at the crime scene. Kirsten filed a restraining order against her husband just a week before she disappeared. Larry also had complete access to the lake house and could have dumped the body without drawing any attention. The evidence supports this and I am going to prove that Larry is guilty.

**Prosecuting-** Elizabeth was having an affair with Larry and it was Elizabeth that wanted Kirsten dead and she is the one who did it. The defense will try to prove otherwise but you the jury will learn the facts and make an accurate, informed decision.

**Judge-** Prosecutor you may call your first witness.

**Prosecutor-** The prosecution calls Harold Manning to the stand.

**Bailiff-** Raise your right hand. Do you swear to tell the truth the whole truth and nothing but the truth so help you God?

**Harold-** I do.

**Bailiff-** You may be seated.

**Prosecutor-** Where were you the night Kirsten was murdered?

**Harold-** I was laid up with severe back pain. I just had surgery, Kirsten was my nurse.

**Prosecutor-** You did some work on Clinton Lake correct? If so, what did you do?

**Harold-** Yes, Gladys owns a house there and I do odd jobs when she is away. That's how I knew Kirsten and her husband. They stayed out there a few times.

**Prosecutor-** Thank you Harold, no further questions your honor.

In the remaining pages of this chapter, you will find a grading rubric that corresponds to the "design-your-own project" format as well as a select few student examples that highlight the variety of ways in which students can present the information learned over the course of the semester. More information about how to use the grading rubric for this assessment can be found in Appendix B.

# FINAL GRADING RUBRIC

Name _____    Score _____ /20 _____ % _____ Grade _____

Choose one of the following as a way to present the evidence for either the Kirsten K. murder or the murder of Larry J.:

(1) Create a concept map showing the chain of events (including evidence from each assessment and motives for each suspect) for the murder
(2) Create a timeline of the murder cases, showing pictures and use of evidence along the timeline.
(3) Create a forensics board, showing pictures of the suspects and victims, including evidence from each assessment that is relevant to each
(4) Create a shoe box model of a recreation of the crime scene from a bird's-eye view for one of the murders including labeled evidence
(5) Write a script for how the court room trial would go for one of the murders (and act it out with classmates)
(6) Create a PowerPoint that would be used in a court case as if you are a forensics specialist called in to testify about the murder
(7) Another approved project by the instructor

## Overall Project Format (Interview about project by teacher)

| Application | # | wgt | Exemplary (10) | At Standard (8) | In Progress (7) | Still Emerging (6) | No Evaluation (0) |
|---|---|---|---|---|---|---|---|
| Communication Skills | | ** | ☐ **Project:** follows a typical forensics case format from the above choices and would help in organizing evidence to solve the case<br>☐ **Presentation to Teacher/Class:** you will be asked to verbally explain your model upon completing the final project<br>☐ **Originality:** your project is unique<br>☐ **Accuracy:** the information in the project is correct | 3 of 4 | 2 of 4 | 1 of 4 | No work shown for this section |

## Evidence Presentation

| Application | # | wgt | Exemplary (10) | At Standard (8) | In Progress (7) | Still Emerging (6) | No Evaluation (0) |
|---|---|---|---|---|---|---|---|
| Connecting Ideas | 1d | ** | Makes insightful connections between ideas or events that might not be obvious; abstract thinking evident (4 of 4)<br>☐ Evidence from each of the 5 assessments were used in the model or write-up<br>☐ Evidence is used to form a believable motive for either the murder of Kirsten K. and Larry J.<br>☐ A connection between the suspects, the motive and evidence is shown by the project chosen<br>☐ The performance assessment number and part is listed with each piece of evidence | Makes general, logical connections between ideas or events; mostly concrete in nature (3 of 4) | Makes superficial connections between ideas; thinking might be confused or incomplete (2 of 4) | Makes incorrect or no connections between ideas (1 of 4) | No work shown for this section |

# Student Project Examples

**STUDENT PROJECT EXAMPLE: CONCEPT MAP**

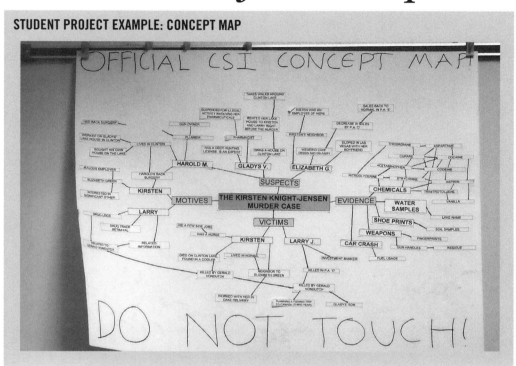

**STUDENT PROJECT EXAMPLE: MURDER TIMELINE**

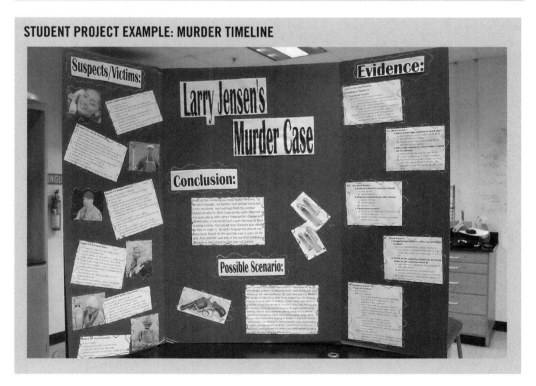

**STUDENT PROJECT EXAMPLE: CONCEPT MAP**

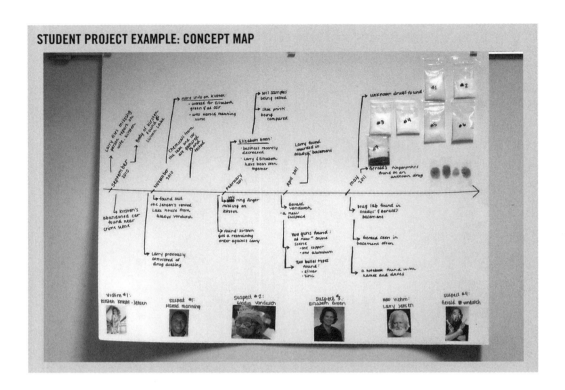

**STUDENT PROJECT EXAMPLE: MURDER TIMELINE**

# Chemistry Concepts Chart

| Title | Topics | Questions Raised | Conclusions |
|---|---|---|---|
| **Performance Assessment #1:**<br><br>**The Cooler and Delivery Truck Evidence** | • density<br>• data interpretation<br>• dimensional analysis (unit conversions)<br>• gas laws<br>• kinetic molecular theory<br>• surface tension | **Part I:**<br>(1) What is the density range of the blue cooler pieces?<br>(2) In which lake should police begin their search for the body?<br>(3) Would the body fit inside the cooler?<br>(4) Would the cooler have been able to float with the body in it, plus a chain wrapped around it?<br>(5) Would the cooler float after water filled it through a bullet hole?<br><br>**Part II:**<br>(1) According to volume data, explain why the police should be able to still get evidence from the delivery truck after retrieving the truck from the lake?<br>(2) Describe the pressure verses volume graph. Use the words *direct or inverse* in your description of the relationship along with data from the graph in your answer to describe which gas law this graph represents.<br>(3) Describe the volume verses temperature graph. Use the words *direct or inverse* in your description of the relationship along with data from the graph in your answer to describe which gas law this graph represents.<br>(4) Using the ideas supporting the kinetic molecular theory, explain why the number of moles of gas in the deployed airbag would stay the same throughout the volume calculations. | **Part I:**<br>(1) Floats in salt water with density of 1.05 g/ml and sinks in vinegar with density of 1.01 g/ml<br>(2) Clinton Lake because its density is 1.05 g/ml and the blue cooler would have floated in this lake but would have sunk in all the other lakes<br>(3) Yes, body would fit in the cooler.<br>(4) Yes, the cooler would only be partially submerged because the displacement height of the water would be less than the height of the cooler.<br>(5) yes, it will still float even if filled with water<br><br>**Part II:**<br>(1) The airbag volume will not go above the maximum 65 Liters as calculated for each of the various depths.<br>(2) The pressure verses volume graph shows an indirect relationship. This shows the relationship in Boyle's Law.<br>(3) The volume verses temperature graph shows a direct relationship. This shows the relationship in Charles' Law.<br>(4) As long as the airbag stays closed and not punctured with holes at all as the delivery truck is being extracted from the lake, the number of moles of gas will stay the same inside the airbag. |

| Title | Topics | Questions Raised | Conclusions |
|---|---|---|---|
| **Performance Assessment #2:**<br><br>**The Chemical Evidence** | • balancing equations<br>• particle/mol/grams calculations<br>• molar mass<br>• stoichiometry<br>• limiting reactants<br>• percent yield<br>• empirical and molecular formulas<br>• percent composition | **Part I:**<br>(1) Based on the percent compositions of chemicals found in the delivery truck and found at the crime scene around the lake, identify the five chemicals.<br><br>**Part II:**<br>(2) Analyze the suspect residues to determine the chemicals that were on the suspects and were also at the crime scene.<br><br>**Part III:**<br>(3) Calculate the amount of moles of each substance that was at the crime scene and in the delivery truck and also found on each of the suspects.<br><br>**Part IV:**<br>(4) Identify the limiting reactant and excess reactant, calculate percent yield, and match any of the unknowns. | **Part I:**<br>Chemical A: vanilla ($C_8H_8O_3$)<br>Chemical B: vanilla ($C_8H_8O_3$)<br>Chemical C: cocaine ($C_{17}H_{21}NO_4$)<br>Chemical D: aspirin ($C_9H_8O_4$)<br>Chemical E: unknown #1 (caffeine: Empirical Formula = $C_4H_5N_2O$)<br><br>**Part II:**<br>Victim's clothing: Kirsten K. has vanilla ($C_8H_8O_3$)<br>Suspect #1: Harold M. has aspirin ($C_9H_8O_4$)<br>Suspect #2: Gladys V. has cocaine ($C_{17}H_{21}NO_4$)<br>Suspect #3: Elizabeth G. has acetaminophen ($C_8H_9NO_2$), unknown #2 (glyoxylic acid: empirical and molecular formula = $C_2H_2O_3$)<br>Suspect #4: Larry J. has nitroglycerine ($C_3H_5N_3O_9$), unknown #1 (caffeine: empirical formula = $C_4H_5N_2O$)<br><br>**Part III:**<br>See student lab report example for work and answers for calculations<br><br>**Part IV:**<br>*Balanced Reaction*<br>$2C_7H_8O_2 + 1C_2H_2O_3 \rightarrow 2C_8H_8O_3 + 1H_2O$<br>limiting reactant = guaiacol, excess reagent = glyoxylic acid<br>theoretical yield = 5.1 g $C_8H_8O_3$<br>percent yield of vanilla = 95.1%, unknown #2 matches glyoxylic acid |

| Title | Topics | Questions Raised | Conclusions |
|-------|--------|------------------|-------------|
| **Performance Assessment #3:**<br><br>**The Nuclear Radiation Evidence** | • concentration<br>• molarity<br>• Beer's law calculations<br>• half-life<br>• carbon dating<br>• radioactive decay of isotopes<br>• nuclear equations | **Part I:**<br>(1) Based on the nitrate soil samples, which suspects can be placed at or near the crime scene?<br><br>**Part II:**<br>(2) Based on the shoeprints, which suspects can be placed at or near the crime scene?<br><br>**Part III:**<br>(3) Using radioactive dating, which bone fragment could be from the victim?<br><br>**Part IV:**<br>(4) Using half-life calculations, what was the time frame of the medical tracer and how much was given to the victim? | **Part I:**<br>(1) Larry and Elizabeth have nitrates found on them that match the nitrates in the soil at the crime scene<br><br>**Part II:**<br>(2) Harold's shoe print was the only shoe print that was not found at the crime scene<br><br>**Part III:**<br>(3) Bone fragment 3 is the only fragment that could belong to the victim because it only has parent isotope in it and has not decayed into any daughter isotope yet; further testing would need to be done by police to determine if the bone fragment actually belongs to the victim, Kirsten K.<br><br>**Part IV:**<br>(4) The victim was given a medical tracer 24 days ago according to the beta decay calculations; the victim was given 34.8 g, which is above the lethal dose of 30.0 g. |

| Title | Topics | Questions Raised | Conclusions |
|---|---|---|---|
| **Performance Assessment #4:**<br><br>**The Weapon Analysis**<br>**Evidence** | • electrochemistry<br>• redox reactions<br>• titrations<br>• molarity<br>• stoichiometry<br>• writing half-reactions<br>• construction of voltaic cells<br>• activity series<br>• pH<br>• acids and bases<br>• titrations | **Part I:**<br>(1) Which suspect's fingerprints are the possible matches to the gun with the aluminum foil handle?<br><br>(2) Which suspect's fingerprints are the possible matches to the gun with the copper handle?<br><br>**Part II:**<br>(3) Which bullet type was able to be matched with which gun and what evidence proves this?<br><br>**Part III:**<br>(4) Which suspect(s) were the positive matches for gun shot residue? Which suspect(s) were the negative matches for the gun shot residue?<br><br>**Part IV:**<br>(5) Which of the suspects and/or victims had stains that fell into the pH range of blood?<br><br>(6) Why may Harold have shown a basic stain and Elizabeth shown an acidic stain? You may have to look back at previous assessments and/or suspect files.<br><br>(7) Which of the suspects/victims did the blood stains prove to match? | **Part I:**<br>(1) Aluminum foil = Larry and Unknown (later introduced in Suspect File D as Gerald)<br><br>(2) Copper handle = Gladys and Unknown (later introduced in Suspect File D as Gerald)<br><br>**Part II:**<br>(3) Aluminum gun with zinc bullet; copper gun with silver bullet<br><br>**Part III:**<br>(4) Positive for gunshot residue = Larry and Gerald; Negative for gunshot residue = Harold, Gladys, and Elizabeth<br><br>**Part IV:**<br>(5) Positive for blood stains = Kirsten, Larry, Gladys, and Gerald<br><br>(6) Harold = plumber and basic cleaners; Elizabeth = glyoxylic acid from baking reaction in PA #2<br><br>(7) Larry = Larry and Gerald;<br>  1. Gerald = Larry, Kirsten, and Gerald; Gladys = Gerald |

| Title | Topics | Questions Raised | Conclusions |
|---|---|---|---|
| **Performance Assessment #5:**<br><br>**The Drug Evidence** | • naming covalent compounds<br>• organic functional groups<br>• infrared spectroscopy<br>• thin layer chromatography<br>• $R_f$ values<br>• solvents and solutions | **Part I:**<br>(1) Can any of the compounds be matched with the unknowns from previous evidence?<br><br>**Part II:**<br>(2) How much total caffeine could be extracted from the coffee found in the plastic tub in the basement?<br><br>**Part III:**<br>(3) Which substances were found in the unknown drug?<br><br>**Part IV:**<br>(4) Which suspect pen(s) match the ink on file in the drug log book? | **Part I:**<br>(1) Spectra A = caffeine;<br>1. Spectra B = aspirin;<br>2. Spectra C = acetaminophen;<br>3. the empirical formula for caffeine matches unknown #2 found at the crime scene and Larry J. from Performance Assessment #1<br><br>**Part II:**<br>(2) Depends on amount students are able to extract; usually student get about 0.1 grams of caffeine from a 100mL sample of coffee solution<br><br>**Part III:**<br>(3) Caffeine and aspirin; combination would be some type of powerful migraine medicine that Gerald/Gladys was making.<br><br>**Part IV:**<br>(4) Pens found on Gladys and Larry match the drug log book. |

# Grading Rubric:
## *Notes to the Teacher and Applications of Learning*

## NOTES TO THE TEACHER

Students are graded for each assessment based on the Illinois State Board of Education (ISBE) Applications of Learning: Solving Problems, Communicating, Using Technology, Working on Teams, and Making Connections (see Applications of Learning Appendix). Not all of the applications of learning are used on each assessment rubric, only the ones that apply. Each section of the lab report is graded individually and has specific check-off points that are listed for students to get full points on each section. Full credit for a section is either 10 points for exemplary work or 5 points if the weight ("wgt") column is weighted by half. If students don't meet all the requirements for a given section, then they may get 8 out of 10 points if they only get 3 of the 4 check-off boxes, or 7 out of 10 points if they only get 2 of the 4 check-off boxes, and so on. Sometimes, if students get half of what one specific check-off box says, then I will mark it a 9.5 or a 7.5.

Along with the assessment handout, students are given the rubric so they know exactly what they have to do to get the grade they want on the assessment. I use this exact rubric to grade the students. Also, if students are given the opportunity to peer evaluate each other's work or correct their assessment, they use this same rubric. At the end of each rubric, I put a Content Recall section. This section ensures that students are completing the assessment based on content we have learned in that unit and not relying on asking me (the instructor) questions as they work through the assessment. If there is a question the group cannot figure out, then they may ask me, but I keep track of who has asked the question and mark the group down to an 8 out of 10 points on that section. Most of the time students find that asking a question to help them understand what they are doing to complete a section of the lab outweighs the 2-point penalty they receive. Students are graded similarly on each assessment; so once they learn the grading system, it becomes easier for them to follow the check-off boxes on the rest of the assessments.

Each of the performance assessments follows the Lab Report Style Guide outline (see Appendix C). Each graded section of the lab report is labeled on the rubric so that students know not only what is graded, but also what the title of each section should be. I have thought about allowing the students to construct a lab report outline together as a class, based on their previous scientific method knowledge. At this point, it makes grading a lot easier to have one rubric for multiple sections of this same class, rather than a separate rubric for each class. I have also thought that it may be beneficial for the students to create their own grading rubric for each assessment. While I think this may increase the level of learning for the students, it is sometimes not practical from a time standpoint, since this assessment already takes approximately a week of class time.

## Applications of Learning Rubric

| Application | # | wgt | Exemplary (10) | At Standard (8) | In Progress (7) | Still Emerging (6) | No Evaluation (0) |
|---|---|---|---|---|---|---|---|
| **A. SOLVING PROBLEMS** | | | | | | | |
| Defining Problems | 1a | * | Definition of problem or issue reflects a broad, insightful view | Definition of problem or issue is reasonable and concise | Definition of problem has aspects that are vague or incomplete | Overall definition of problem is vague or unreasonable | No work shown for this section |
| Problem Calculations | 2a | * | All essential information is evident through well-organized work while justifying the solution | Most essential information is evident through organized work while leading to the solution | Minimum information is evident through work with a solution present | Work is extremely unorganized with no solution present | No work shown for this section |
| Making Conclusions | 3a | * | Implications of ideas or information (conclusions) extend in multiple directions—abstract or big picture thinking evident when appropriate | Implications of ideas or information are general and logical | Implications of ideas or information are illogical or unreasonable to some degree, but sound overall | Implications of ideas or information are illogical or unreasonable overall; little understanding is evident | No work shown for this section |
| **B. COMMUNICATING** | | | | | | | |
| Interpreting Models | 1b | * | Interprets visuals or models at a complex level | Interprets visuals or models at a general level | Interpretation of visuals or models contains errors that restrict understanding | Shows fundamental errors in use and understanding of visuals | No work shown for this section |
| Organization | 2b | * | Assignment is organized, flows together well, and is of high quality visually | Assignment is organized, complete, and generally presentable | Parts of assignment are disorganized, incomplete, or of low quality | Significant parts of the assignment are missing or are cluttered | No work shown for this section |
| Supporting Ideas | 3b | * | Support used is varied, the best available, and strongly enhances audience understanding | Support is accurate and sufficiently detailed—all basics evident | Support is insufficient, inaccurate, or vague in places—enough to confuse audience somewhat | Support is missing, inaccurate, or vague overall | No work shown for this section |
| **C. USING TECHNOLOGY** | | | | | | | |
| Technology Applicatioins | 1c | * | Technology used is best available and appropriate for the required research, data representation, interpretation, and communication of results | Technology was used for the required research, data representation, interpretation, and communication of results | Technology used was insufficient for the required research, data representation, and communication of results | Evidence of technology use is missing and/or insufficient | No work show for this section |
| **D. MAKING CONNECTIONS** | | | | | | | |
| Connecting Ideas | 1d | * | Makes insightful connections between ideas or events that might not be obvious—abstract thinking evident | Makes general, logical connections between ideas or events—mostly concrete in nature | Makes superficial connections between ideas—thinking might be confused or incomplete | Makes incorrect or no connections between ideas | No work shown for this section |
| **E. WORKING IN TEAMS** | | | | | | | |
| Team Evaluations | 1e | * | Works effectively in a group setting by willingly participating and positively contributing without being continually asked by the team to remain on task | Works in a group setting participating and contributing when asked to by the team, and remains on task most of the time | Contributes minimally to the group, has to continually be asked to participate by the team, and is oftentimes off task | Does not contribute to the group at all, is offtask, and has to be continually reminded what the task is | No team evaluation was turned in |
| **F. CONTENT and INDEPENDENCE** | | | | | | | |
| Content Recall | 1f | * | Recalls virtually all essential terms and factual information and 0 content questions asked to instructor | Recalls most essential terms and factual information and 1 content question asked to instructor | Recalls a minimum of essential terms and factual information and 2 content questions asked to instructor | Recalls virtually no essential terms and factual information and 3 or more content questions asked to instructor | No work shown for this section |

# Lab Report Style Guide

## GENERAL GUIDELINES:

- Lab Reports will be compiled and submitted individually (no lab book). **All lab reports should be typed**.
- If typing a lab report is an issue, the lab template provided should be used and should be discussed with the teacher in advance.
- Expect at least one formal lab report each quarter.
- A scientific lab report must be written in complete sentences.
- **DO NOT USE** personal pronouns. For example, instead of saying "We set up two beakers, one next to the other," you would say, "Two beakers were set up, one next to the other." Instead of saying, "Tom measured the height of the liquid. It was 2.0 cm," you would say, "The height of the liquid was measured to be 2.0 cm."

## OUTLINE FORMAT

### Title

I.  Introduction
    a.  Background Information
    b.  Purpose
    c.  Hypothesis
    d.  Procedure
    e.  Materials Used
II. Data
    a.  Data Tables From Observations
III. Analysis
    a.  Graphs of Data
    b.  Calculations
        i.  Data Calculations
        ii. Percent Error or Percent Difference Calculations
IV. Conclusion
V.  Discussion Questions

**Suggestion:** Type this outline format into your computer and save it as a template, then just fill in the sections for each separate lab report.

## *EXPLANATIONS BY SECTIONS*

## TITLE PAGE

Each Report shall include a separate title page. It should include the title of the lab centered on the page. The student's name, teacher's name, course, class period, and the date of submission should appear in the lower right corner of the page.

## I. INTRODUCTION

The introduction will include five separate sections. For each lab, information required in the pre-lab will be specified.

### BACKGROUND INFORMATION

- o   What is already known about this topic? Gather as much information and detail as possible before and throughout the experiment through **research** or **observations**.

### PURPOSE

- o   What is the point of doing this lab? What is supposed to be known when the lab is completed? Make sure this section is in your own words.

### HYPOTHESIS

- o   What could the right answer be? What could happen throughout the lab?
- o   Should be written as an "If…then" statement
- o   The prediction must be a concise, one-sentence statement that is TESTABLE in reference to the purpose defined.
- o   The predictions should NOT start with "The hypothesis is…" or start with "I think…".

### PROCEDURE

- o   What steps will be taken to solve the issue? How will the information be collected and recorded?
- o   The procedure will be numbered, in order of how each step will be performed with no more than one instruction per step. Example:
  1.
  2.
- o   Each instruction must be specific. For example, stating exactly what data is to be collected, how often, and how it is to be analyzed and recorded.
- o   If the procedure is given to you in the lab work, you only have to note any changes to the procedure and do NOT have to retype the entire procedure.

## MATERIALS USED
o   Include both a list of materials and a diagram of the equipment when appropriate.

# II. DATA

This section will include a record of the measurements taken, plus anything that was observed during the investigation. Any required tables for measurements should be prepared before beginning the lab if possible. Anything that differs from what is expected, or which could affect results, should be noted here. For example, "Some friction was experienced causing the ticker tape not to run smoothly through the guides."

### OBSERVATIONS IN A DATA TABLE OR CHART
o   Anything that differs from what is expected, or anything that could affect results, should be noted in this section.
o   The data presented visually will often appear in the form of a table or chart of values.
o   The table/chart must be clearly labeled, including all units and a relevant title.
o   This section must be well organized and show trends.
o   Measured quantities should be separate from the calculated values.

# III. ANALYSIS

o   Restate **all data** in paragraph form.
o   State any trends the data shows in the data tables and/or graphs.

### GRAPHS
o   Graphs will be computer generated.
o   All graphs must include complete title and labeled axes, including units and scale.
o   Points must be properly plotted and best-fit curves or lines carefully drawn to show trends.

### CALCULATIONS
**Data Calculations**
o   Any work should be shown for: all calculations performed to find any data in a table or a graph; any calculations that helped to make the lab's conclusion.

**Percent Error and Percent Difference Calculations**
o   *Percent Error*
    When an experimental value is compared to a KNOWN value that has a standard value, we calculate a percent error assuming that we are some amount "off" the given value.
    % Error may either be positive (the experimental result is too high) or negative (the experimental result is too low).

$$\% \text{ Error } = \frac{(\text{Experimental Value}) - (\text{Theoretical Value})}{(\text{Theoretical Value})} \times 100$$

o ***Percent Difference***

When we perform an experiment in which we do not have a KNOWN value, we calculate a percent difference between two measured values. As we do not know the "right" answer, we calculate the percent the two values are different. % Difference may either be positive (the original result is too high) or negative (the original result is too low)…if original value is Value 1.

$$\% \text{ Difference} = \frac{(\text{Value 1}) - (\text{Value 2})}{(\text{Average of Value 1 and Value 2})} \times 100$$

## IV. CONCLUSION

o This is a summary of what the investigation showed.
o It should answer the purpose of the lab. For example, if the purpose was "… to measure the concentration of a solution" then the conclusion should be something like, "…the concentration of the solution was measured to be .5m."
o Support any statements with DATA.
o Mention of % error or % difference should also be included here if applicable.
o Only significant data should be highlighted, not all data.

## V. DISCUSSION QUESTIONS

o Often the discussion questions will be guided by postlab questions.
  • If no discussion questions are present, then this section is not required.

# *Forensic Tags*

Forensics Evidence Tag

**Description of item:**

_____
_____
_____

**Location of collection:**

_____
_____

**Additional information:**

_____
_____
_____

Forensics Evidence Tag

**Description of item:**

_____
_____
_____

**Location of collection:**

_____
_____

**Additional information:**

_____
_____
_____

Forensics Evidence Tag

**Description of item:**

_____
_____
_____

**Location of collection:**

_____
_____

**Additional information:**

_____
_____
_____

Forensics Evidence Tag

**Description of item:**

_____
_____
_____

**Location of collection:**

_____
_____

**Additional information:**

_____
_____
_____

Forensics Evidence Tag

**Description of item:**

_____
_____
_____

**Location of collection:**

_____
_____

**Additional information:**

_____
_____
_____

Forensics Evidence Tag

**Description of item:**

_____
_____
_____

**Location of collection:**

_____
_____

**Additional information:**

_____
_____
_____

Forensics Evidence Tag

**Description of item:**

_____
_____
_____

**Location of collection:**

_____
_____

**Additional information:**

_____
_____

Forensics Evidence Tag

**Description of item:**

_____
_____
_____

**Location of collection:**

_____
_____

**Additional information:**

_____
_____

# Sample Inquiry Lab

This appendix contains a sample inquiry unit that is used at the beginning of the year to refresh students' chemistry content, introduce inquiry-based activities, and provide an introduction to the forensics performance-based assessments that students will be completing throughout the year. The unit plan includes a timeline, as well as descriptions of the stations used in the activities, centering on a murder mystery case involving Dr. BrINClHOF and the topic of climate change.

## UNIT OUTLINE AND BACKGROUND INFORMATION

### Day 1

Chemistry II students learn that Dr. BrINClHOF (an acronym for diatomic elements introduced in first-year chemistry) has been murdered in the lab. I come running down the hall after the bell has rung, approaching my students who are standing outside my room, which is covered with police tape. I inform them that police need their help in determining what Dr. BrINClHOF was studying in our lab and how it might have contributed to his demise. Students are asked to not touch anything as they tour the crime scene. Each station is already set up as if that lab had already been completed by Dr. BrINClHOF, and students take notes on what they see at each station.

### Day 2

Students finish taking notes about their observations at each station, drawing clues from each station to determine what Dr. BrINClHOF was studying prior to his murder.

### Days 3–4

Each student group draws a station number and then focuses on that specific lab station. Students are asked to recreate that specific lab as a demo to the class by working backward from the end result that they see. Students must figure out what aspects of that lab have to do with the overall "big" topic Dr. BrINClHOF was studying.

### Day 5

New evidence suggests that Dr. BrINClHOF has hidden other clues around the school because he was receiving threats from radical environmentalists and other local scientists about the nature of his study. Students use a GPS system to locate the hidden messages at various places around the school, adding this information to the other clues to figure out what Dr. BrINClHOF was studying before his death.

### Day 6

Students work in the computer lab to develop a presentation of their findings to show as part of their demo to the class. Students also have to develop a conclusion as to what Dr. BrINClHOF was studying and support it with evidence from the lab stations visited on Day 1 and Day 2. They also have to connect their conclusion with their specific lab.

### Days 7–9

Use these days for student presentations and evaluations.

### Day 10

Use this day to wrap up and explain how this activity leads into the yearlong forensics investigation the students are going to be doing, with each of the five performance assessments for each Chemistry II content unit. This idea of thinking backward from what is observed at a crime scene will be used in the forensics curriculum to connect smaller pieces of evidence to the big picture of what is happening among suspects.

### Assessment

This assessment can be used as a hands-on pretest to see what students remember about the scientific method, lab procedures, equipment, lab safety, graphing techniques, and various Chemistry I topics such as gas laws, electromagnetic spectrum, density, states of matter, molecular masses, and atomic theory. This assessment will also serve as an introduction to new topics in Chemistry II such as atmospheric pressure, kinetic molecular theory, and advanced gas laws calculations.

## STATION ACTIVITIES OUTLINE AND HIDDEN MESSAGES

Included in the following pages are brief outlines of the activities at each station as well as some hidden message cards that are placed throughout the school. Many of the stations used in this lab are common gas laws demonstrations.

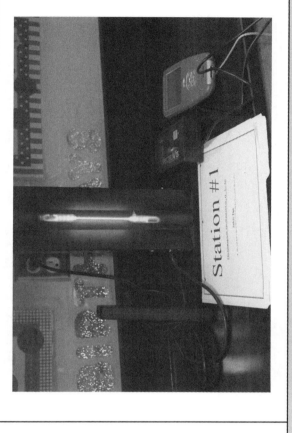

## STATION 1

**Activity:** Electromagnetic Spectrum of $CO_2$, Air

**Description:** Students are testing the electromagnetic spectrum of various gas samples using Lab Quest technology with light sensors; students will understand how the spectra are different and have to explain why they are different using atomic theory from Chemistry I

**National Science Education Standards:** *Content Standard A: Science as Inquiry; Content Standard B: Physical Science; Content Standard E: Science in Personal and Social Perspectives; Content Standard G: History and Nature of Science*

**Resources:** energy source, various gas tubes, Lab Quest, light sensor

**Global Climate Change Connection:** the spectra of the gases viewed by the students are of atmospheric gases that are either known greenhouse gases or naturally occur in the air

## STATION 2

**Activity:** $CO_2$ Flame Test-Density of Gases

**Description:** Students will generate $CO_2$ by mixing baking soda and vinegar in the bottom of a 2L bottle. Then using a wire holder, they lower a candle down into the $CO_2$ gas and the flame will go out. Students will then pour $CO_2$ gas from one bottle to another using the candle as a tester to see the height of $CO_2$ change from one bottle to another.

**National Science Education Standards:** *Content Standard A: Science as Inquiry; Content Standard B: Physical Science; Content Standard E: Science in Personal and Social Perspectives; Content Standard G: History and Nature of Science*

**Resources:** Two 2L bottles, votive candles, baking soda, vinegar, wire holder, clear tubing, clear plastic container, bubble solution, blower.

**Global Climate Change Connection:** focusing on the properties of $CO_2$ as a greenhouse gas

## STATION 3

**Activity:** Candle Heights–Density of Gases

**Description:** Students will cover three burning candles of different heights and predict which candle will go out first. Then students will do a second experiment where they generate $CO_2$ with dry ice or with baking soda and vinegar and test the movement of $CO_2$ in a container with 3 candles of different heights to see which candle goes out first. Students will pour the $CO_2$ into the open container to test their predictions and then explain the differences between the experiment.

**National Science Education Standards:** *Content Standard A: Science as Inquiry; Content Standard B: Physical Science; Content Standard E: Science in Personal and Social Perspectives; Content Standard G: History and Nature of Science*

**Resources:** Three candles of different heights/preburned, baking soda, vinegar, large container

**Global Climate Change Connection:** focusing on the properties of $CO_2$ as a greenhouse gas.

## STATION 4

**Activity:** Candle Snuffing–Density of Gases

**Description:** Students will produce $CO_2$ gas by mixing baking soda and vinegar, and then pour the $CO_2$ gas down a tube with lighted candles at various points within the tube. Students will see the result of the $CO_2$ moving down the tube by watching the candles go out one by one as the $CO_2$ gets to them

**National Science Education Standards:** *Content Standard A: Science as Inquiry; Content Standard B: Physical Science; Content Standard E: Science in Personal and Social Perspectives; Content Standard G: History and Nature of Science*

**Resources:** Flinn Kit "Seeing the Invisible"

**Global Climate Change Connection:** focusing on the properties of $CO_2$ as a greenhouse gas

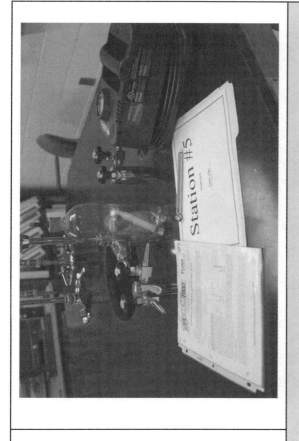

## STATION 5

**Activity:** Boyle's Law; Generate Graph of P vs V

**Description:** Air is pumped into the bottle and an initial volume reading of the syringe is taken. Air is released from the bottle using a tire gauge. The tire gauge is also used to take pressure readings in the bottle along with the changing volume readings in the syringe. Students are able to form a data table and graph from the data.

**National Science Education Standards:** *Content Standard A: Science as Inquiry; Content Standard B: Physical Science; Content Standard E: Science in Personal and Social Perspectives; Content Standard G: History and Nature of Science*

**Resources:** Flinn Syringe in bottle setup with tire pump lid

**Global Climate Change Connection:** understanding factors that affect gases through gas law relationships

## STATION 6

**Activity:** Charles' Law and Absolute Zero: Syringe of Air; Generate Graph of T vs V

**Description:** The students will put the same syringe in different beakers of different solutions in order to see how temperature change affects the volume of air in the syringe. Students are able to form a data table and graph from the data collected in this lab exercise.

**National Science Education Standards:** *Content Standard A: Science as Inquiry; Content Standard B: Physical Science; Content Standard E: Science in Personal and Social Perspectives; Content Standard G: History and Nature of Science*

**Resources:** salt/cold/warm water solutions, syringes, and thermometer

**Global Climate Change Connection:** understanding factors that affect gases through gas law relationships

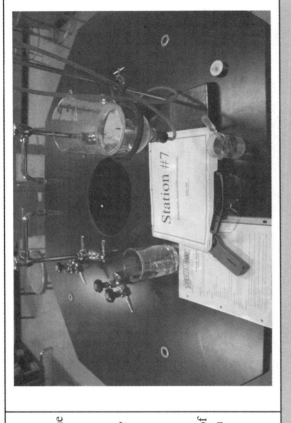

## STATION 7

**Activity:** Methane Mamba-Density of Gases and Hydrocarbons

**Description:** Students will watch as the methane gas goes through the soap solution to form a tower of bubbles. They will also notice that sometimes parts of the tower of bubbles can float up to the ceiling.

**National Science Education Standards:** *Content Standard A: Science as Inquiry; Content Standard B: Physical Science; Content Standard E: Science in Personal and Social Perspectives; Content Standard G: History and Nature of Science*

**Resources:** half 2L bottle setup with stopper and hose to methane gas source, liquid soap solution, lighter

**Global Climate Change Connection:** focusing on the properties of $CH_4$ as a greenhouse gas and also understand the term *hydrocarbon* and how it is used in CFCs within the greenhouse gases

## STATION 8

**Activity:** Rates of Diffusion-KMT

**Description:** Students place the concentrated solutions on the end of a cotton swab, and then place each end of the swab in a clear straw. The gases of each of the concentrated solutions will meet closer to the heavier gas and form a white circle to help explain how gases with different molecular weights will move differently within space.

**National Science Education Standards:** *Content Standard A: Science as Inquiry; Content Standard B: Physical Science; Content Standard E: Science in Personal and Social Perspectives; Content Standard G: History and Nature of Science*

**Resources:** clear straws, ammonium hydroxide (14.8 M), hydrochloric acid (12 M)

**Global Climate Change Connection:** focus on the movement of gases depends on their molecular masses

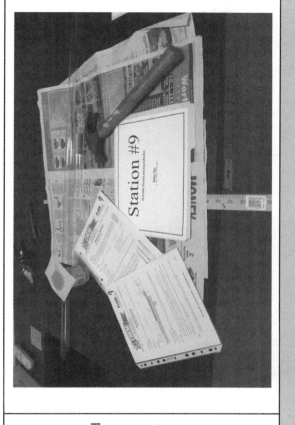

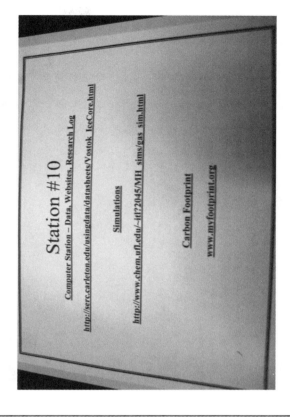

## STATION 9

**Activity:** Hydraulic Elevator and Board Breaker—Atmospheric Pressure

**Description:** In the hydraulic elevator, a test tube is placed in water-filled tube and then inverted so it moves to the top. The board breaker involves newspaper over a meter stick hanging over the edge of a table, broken with just the newspaper and a hammer.

**National Science Education Standards:** *Content Standard A: Science as Inquiry; Content Standard B: Physical Science; Content Standard E: Science in Personal and Social Perspectives; Content Standard G: History and Nature of Science*

**Resources:** newspaper, meter stick, tubing/stopper/colored water, plastic tubing 2-4 cm in diameter

**Global Climate Change Connection:** understanding atmospheric pressure to understand greenhouse gases

## STATION 10

**Activity:** Computer Station—Data *http://serc.carleton.edu/ usingdata/datasheets/Vostok_IceCore.html, simulations www.chem. ufl.edu/~itl/2045/MH_sims/gas_sim.html,* and carbon footprint (*www.myfootprint.org*)

**Description:** Students investigate these websites looking at data that Dr. BrINCIHOF was analyzing to help determine what exactly he was studying, manipulating online gas law setups, and calculating carbon footprints.

**National Science Education Standards:** *Content Standard A: Science as Inquiry; Content Standard B: Physical Science; Content Standard E: Science in Personal and Social Perspectives; Content Standard G: History and Nature of Science*

**Resources:** laptop computer/website

**Global Climate Change Connection:** Use of the Vostok ice core $CO_2$ data to study the relationship between $CO_2$ levels and temperature, understanding how students directly contribute to global climate change.

| Hidden Message #1 |
| --- |

## Graph 1: CO₂ Levels and Temperature Change Over the Past 400,000 Years

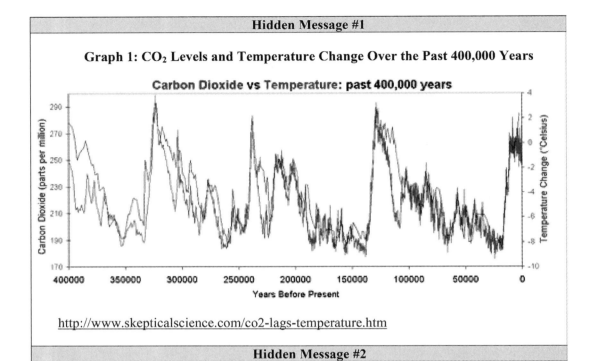

http://www.skepticalscience.com/co2-lags-temperature.htm

| Hidden Message #2 |
| --- |

## Graph 2: Recent Fossil Fuel Emissions

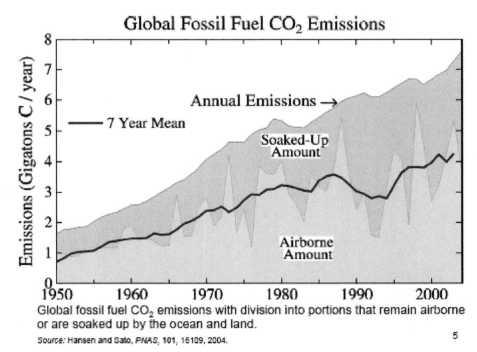

Global fossil fuel CO₂ emissions with division into portions that remain airborne or are soaked up by the ocean and land.

Source: Hansen and Sato, *PNAS*, 101, 16109, 2004.

http://chartsgraphs.wordpress.com/2009/09/11/co2-emissions-changes-in-atmospheric-levels/

## Hidden Message #3

### Graph 3: Carbon Dioxide Concentrations

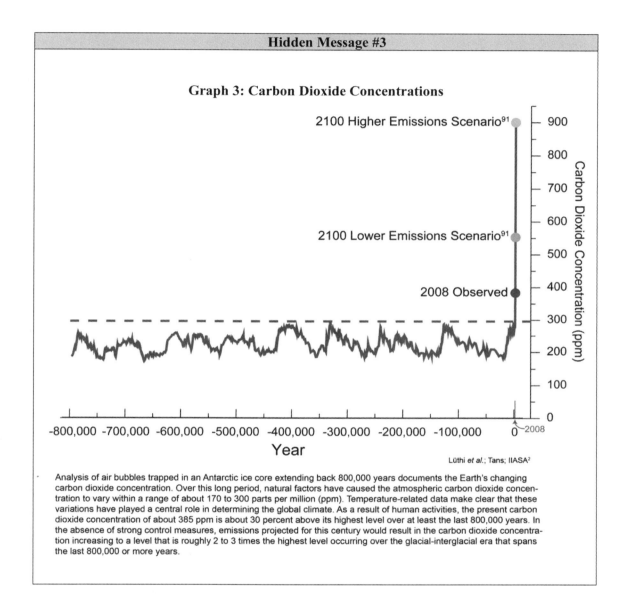

Lüthi *et al.*; Tans; IIASA[2]

Analysis of air bubbles trapped in an Antarctic ice core extending back 800,000 years documents the Earth's changing carbon dioxide concentration. Over this long period, natural factors have caused the atmospheric carbon dioxide concentration to vary within a range of about 170 to 300 parts per million (ppm). Temperature-related data make clear that these variations have played a central role in determining the global climate. As a result of human activities, the present carbon dioxide concentration of about 385 ppm is about 30 percent above its highest level over at least the last 800,000 years. In the absence of strong control measures, emissions projected for this century would result in the carbon dioxide concentration increasing to a level that is roughly 2 to 3 times the highest level occurring over the glacial-interglacial era that spans the last 800,000 or more years.

| Hidden Message #4 |
|---|

**Global climate change debate gets local and ugly**
Indignant scientist threatens Bloomington-Normal critic with libel suit — and he doesn't stop there
Pantagraph
Updated: 07/24/2010 04:10:53 PM CDT

A Bloomington-Normal professor, Dr. BrINClHOF, touched off a bitter dispute when he posted an online slideshow rebutting a speech by a local climate change skeptic, a cyber flap that's resulted in harsh words and threats of legal action.

John Abraham, a professor of thermal sciences at Illinois State University, said Friday he decided he had a responsibility as a scientist to challenge remarks Dr. BrINClHOF made during a speech last October at ISU in Felmley Hall.

"He presented science that was at odds with the understanding of the vast majority of people working in the field," Abraham said. "The problem with that is that people who listened to his presentation would come away with a misconception about what is known about climate change and what a serious issue this is."

Dr. BrINClHOF, a third generation scientist in his family, said he was libeled. He fired back with letters to ISU officials, including its president, Dr. Al Bowman, demanding that Abraham be disciplined. He also issued a 99-page rebuttal.

Abraham said he was gratified by the support he's received from scientists around the world.

A lawyer for the school, Phyllis Karasov, wrote to Dr. BrINClHOF last month saying Abraham "has done nothing improper or illegal" and he "has not engaged in any academic or professional misconduct."

She wrote that there would be no investigation, retraction or apology.

And she threatened "appropriate legal action" if Dr. BrINClHOF continued making "disparaging or defamatory comments" about the university, Bowman, Abraham, or anyone else associated with the school.

Abraham said scientists must convey the message that there's a strong consensus within the scientific community that climate change is a real problem because much of the public has the mistaken impression there isn't.

He declined to comment on his views about the viscount, saying he found all the name-calling "completely uninteresting."

"But what it says to me is this topic has somehow become way too divisive and far too polarizing," Abraham said. "And as long it's polarized in this way, we are incapable as a society of coming together and making the tough decisions we've got to make."

## Hidden Message #5

## Hidden Message #6

Reflected by Earth's Surface to Space

Some Longwave is Lost to Space

Some Longwave is Lost to Space

**Greenhouse Gases**

Solar Energy Absorbed at Surface

Converted into Heat Causing the Emission of Longwave Radiation

Surface Gains More Heat and Longwave Radiation is Emitted Again

Surface Gains More Heat and Longwave Radiation is Emitted Again

## Hidden Message #7

### Animals Struggle With Effects of Global Climate Change

As temperatures rise, climate change creates challenges for the world's fauna.

**A VARIETY OF RESPONSES**

**Shifting Habitats**
The American pika, a small rodent that lives in California mountains, cannot tolerate temperatures much higher than 80 degrees. As temperatures have risen, some pika populations have moved more than 1,300 feet further up the slopes to find a cooler home.

**Predators Decline as Prey Declines**
On Isle Royale, Mich., higher temperatures mean that one species of tick is growing more numerous and becoming more troublesome for the island's moose. As the population of moose has declined, so has the population of wolves, which prey on the moose for food.

**Shifting Migration Patterns**
Many birds have begun making their annual migrations earlier — some British species have shifted by two to three weeks over the past 30 years. That can be a problem if the bird's main food source doesn't also shift its timing so it is available when the bird needs to eat.

**Entire Ecosystem Changes**
In the northern Bering Sea, near Alaska, warmer waters are causing an entire ecosystem shift. Native animals, such as walruses and gray whales, are finding less of the prey animals they rely on. At the same time, fish are moving in from less frigid areas.

**Adaptation**
Research on wood frogs in New England seems to show that they may be able to evolve and adapt to rising temperatures. That is good news, but scientists say that many animals will not be able to evolve in the same way.

**CHANGES LOCAL AND BEYOND**

**Blackwater National Wildlife Refuge, Md.**
Rising water levels threaten to turn most of this enormous swamp — which shelters baby fish and blue crabs along with migrating birds — into open water by 2030. A crucial habitat on the Eastern Shore could vanish.

**Catoctin Mountain, Frederick County**
The brook trout that live in mountain streams here cannot tolerate water much hotter than 68 degrees. As temperatures rise, the fish in central Maryland could be gone in a century.

**Monteverde Cloud Forest, Costa Rica**
Animals living in this forest depend on moisture from near-constant clouds of mist and fog. Climate change seems to be reducing this moisture. Two amphibian species have not been seen since the 1980s and are now presumed extinct.

**South Pacific Ocean**
Warming waters have become too hot for coral reefs in some places, leading to so-called "bleachings" in which large amounts of coral die. During 1998, warm temperatures killed off about 16 percent of all the world's coral.

**Beaufort and Chukchi seas, off Alaska**
Walrus mothers in this area typically leave their young on the sea ice while they dive down to find food on the bottom. But now, sea ice is melting more rapidly than before, which can leave walrus calves floating helplessly in open water.

GRAPHIC:David Farenthold And Patterson Clark - The Washington Post - September 15, 2007

**Hidden Message #8**

# Most Americans Believe Global Warming Exists

51%    29%    15%    3%

- 51% believe climate change is caused by human activities
- 29% believe it's occurring naturally
- 15% believe it needs to be proven scientifically either way
- 3% believe it doesn't exist

**enviromedia®**
SOCIAL MARKETING

Commissioned by EnviroMedia Social Marketing (enviromedia.com).
Survey of 1,000 Americans by Opinion Research Corporation Jan. 23-26, 2009.
Margin of error +/- 3.2%.

*Page numbers printed in **boldface** type refer to figures or tables.*